written in Jest!

Written in Jest!

WAY-OUT APPLICATIONS
FOR IMPROBABLE JOBS

MICHAEL A. LEE

ROBSON BOOKS

First published in Great Britain in 2002 by Robson Books, 64 Brewery Road,
London N7 9NT

A member of **Chrysalis** Books plc

Copyright © 2002 Michael A. Lee

British Library Cataloguing in Publication Data
A catalogue record for this book is available from the British Library

ISBN 1 86105 577 3

Typeset by SX Composing DTP, Rayleigh, Essex
Printed by Bell & Bain Ltd, Glasgow

To my wife Ann-Marie and my two sons,
Tom and George

MICHAEL PALIN
Somewhere in London

Michael A. Lee
Somewhere in West Yorkshire

10th January 2002

Dear Michael Lee,

I've now had time to look through the letters and replies you sent me, and I must say they made me laugh a great deal. I think there is something intrinsically funny about the relentlessness of your quest to be these various strange things, and I also like the somewhat obsessive use of certain qualifications, e.g. fell running, to bait the hook.

But what makes it work for me, apart from your creative approach, are the length and detail of some of the replies. There are clearly a lot of very bored people in offices, doctors' surgeries and Lambeth Palaces around the country who have been stirred to imaginative replies by your own batty approach. The joke builds very well the more you read, and I think in the right hands it could make a very funny book indeed.

All good wishes, and apologies for not having really had time to savour the letters the first time round.

Yours,

Michael Palin

PS Do you really exist?

INTRODUCTION

It all began in October 2000. I had only recently turned forty and, like thousands of other men at this awkward phase of life, had decided my career was only partially addressing my needs and interests, and that it was high time I took some positive action to change my daily priorities and perspectives. As something of a country music fan, enjoying many of the old favourite ballads, such as Marty Robbins' 'El Paso', it was quite obvious to me that what I needed to do was to apply to become Mayor of the town featured in a foot-tapping cowboy song. So that's what I did.

A letter was sent to the town hall in El Paso, Texas and within it, a glowing self-appraisal presenting a good case for my becoming the next Mayor. Whether or not El Paso actually *needed* a new Mayor was not something I had particularly considered, but I posted the application anyway and then duly forgot all about it, and continued with my long-standing work and social routines. At least that was the story for three weeks . . .

And then, late one night, the phone rang. 'Hi there, Mr Lee. This is Suzanne Michaels of CBS Channel 4 News in El Paso, Texas ringing with regard to your application to be the next Mayor. In relation to the forthcoming spring elections the Town Hall has passed on a copy of your letter to us and we were interested to contact you. How did you first hear about our elections and why would an Englishman living in England want to be the Mayor of an American city where 80 per cent of the 750,000 population is of Hispanic origin anyway?'

'Oh, ah, yes,' I eloquently replied. 'Well, you see, I didn't actually know there were any elections about to take place but of the three types of people you might have applying to be Mayor: those that make things happen, those that watch things happen and those that ask, "What happened?" I would be someone who could make things happen and ensure El Paso becomes a better place for everyone. Why do you ask?'

I was a little fazed at such late-night questions for which I had a lack of prepared answers but felt I was surviving the situation reasonably well so far. 'Mr Lee, in sixty minutes we are broadcasting a Spring Election programme to the local population and as our sixth Mayoral candidate it would be great to have some background relating to your interest and abilities. Also, would it be possible for you to send a photo of yourself attached to an e-mail and we will broadcast your picture along with your comments?'

'I see,' I said. 'That's fine. I'll send the photo right away and I'm only too happy to answer any questions you have for me. Incidentally, I didn't realise that El Paso was so large. In the old song that inspired me to write I had the impression of a one-street town with a Sheriff's office, a saloon and a jail. It sounds like the place is a tad bigger! Does Felina still live there?'

As a consequence of our telephone conversation my face was seen and my Yorkshire accent heard by hundreds of thousands of people around Texas and as it turned out, in parts of Mexico too! Despite the fact that I could not technically run for Mayor without living in the City as a US resident for at least a year, fame had nevertheless finally crossed my threshold and I was now something of a celebrity, be it in a rather limited capacity. Unlike Andy Warhol's suggestion that everyone is famous for fifteen minutes, my time frame could be measured in seconds. However, it was interesting to observe that due to a moment of madness or creative letter writing, or whatever else one would like to call a fleeting desire to be a Texan mayor, a seed of an idea was planted deep in the core of my convoluted brain and began to grow there. As the seed grew, so roots were planted in the stuff of imagination and various shoots of opportunity started to appear . . .

My wife suggested I could be showing the first signs of insanity and it might be a good idea to suppress such unconventional thinking for the sake of comfort and security, but I disagreed with her. My mind was made up. I would begin writing letters of application for jobs that were either impossibly beyond my capability or for which I would be deemed massively under-qualified or under-skilled, or for jobs that don't exist at all but just possibly might, if reality were viewed from a different angle. I would collect the replies, put together a bestselling book and perhaps become a wealthy author and lecturer in no time at all. I would then have more time for my wife and my two fine sons, an opportunity to enjoy more fell running and gardening, and the money to drink as many Guinnesses as I would wish, without counting the cost. In short, within a few days I had become a man with a mission. Initially I experienced the odd moment of doubt about my unusual endeavours. 'You should not write letters of that kind to the British Special Forces,' my wife scolded one day. 'First of all, they might take offence at your insolence and have you arrested or shot and secondly, even if they don't, whoever heard of a person applying to be a regimental mascot?'

I did worry about the 'being shot' suggestion, especially when there was nothing but silence from the Special Air Service or Royal Marine Commandos, but when at last a reply arrived from the Parachute Regimental Association in a style of obvious appreciation and humour, I was fired up with enthusiasm and self-confidence. For a short time I actually believed I would become the next mascot!

Throughout the following pages you will read various letters of application to a variety of organisations and institutions, societies and federations, businesses and individuals and indeed, a host of wonderful responses. Of the many, many letters compiled and posted during the last few months I have been interested to note that 75 per cent of them received a reply and of these a substantial number are written in a manner which has restored my faith in the presence and power of humour.

Even when humour has not been high on the agenda of the person replying to a letter, it has still surfaced in the way in which obvious madness, sarcasm and sheer brass neck has been purposefully ignored for the sake of political correctness, process or laziness. In itself this can be rather amusing. Within these pages are great lessons in lateral thinking, communication styles, pursuing unusual opportunities and perhaps elements of challenging convention. Most of all there is the enjoyment of a jolly good belly-splitting laugh.

The majority of the following letters are accompanied by their replies. Where there is no reply to read you may assume none was received but imagination may run riot wondering what the replies could have been. How would you have replied? What would you have said? There is an old proverb, 'A merry heart maketh good medicine'. I believe most of you reading these letters will find your mouth turning up at the corners and experience a little levity and lifting of spirits. A page or two read on the Tube or a plane may put into context the stresses and strains of the day ahead, or the day just endured. My guess is that you will begin to consider the sorts of curious roles you could apply for if you were to explore your own creative masterpieces.

Several people have asked me the question, 'What would you do if you were offered one of the jobs you have applied for?' The answer is simple: I would accept it. What better than being remembered as 'Jack the Giant Killer [the Second]', 'The Beast of Bodmin Moor' or the officially recognised hairy Dulux dog? I would grasp the chance to work for the French Navy as a Submarine Periscope Polishing Executive or indeed, as Principal Prodder and Nudge-Master at the House of Lords. To this day I would enjoy nothing better than being the modern-day Witchfinder General! So please read on . . .

Somewhere in West Yorkshire
26 October 2000

The Commanding Officer
Headquarters
The Parachute Regiment
Aldershot GU11 2BY
Hampshire

Dear Sir

I am writing to you a most unusual letter, namely to apply for the position of 'Regimental Mascot' should that vacancy become available in the near future.

It has always struck me as a rather unusual quirk of many British army regiments to have as a mascot an animal of some non-human kind to parade alongside some of the best trained and most professional soldiers in the world.

Would it not be better instead to employ for a modest sum of money a human mascot such as myself to march, without lead or handler, in a respected fashion dressed in suitable mascot attire along with the troops at various events and offer a human perspective to the role?

Aged 40, I am a seasoned fell-runner so exceptionally fit for my age, educated to degree standard, and though it is quite some time since I donned a uniform I am told by my long-suffering wife I can be a rather dapper chap in a rugged sort of way. If as mascot I am required to dance or sing, this too I am capable of though I would probably require a ration of alcohol beforehand.

In summary I would make an ideal mascot for the Parachute Regiment and look forward to hearing from you reference the appropriate application/interview process.

Sincerely

Michael A. Lee

UTRINQUE PARATUS

AD UNUM OMNES

THE PARACHUTE REGIMENTAL ASSOCIATION

Patron: HIS ROYAL HIGHNESS THE PRINCE OF WALES, KG, KT, PC, GCB, AK, QSO, ADC

BROWNING BARRACKS
ALDERSHOT, GU11 2BU
HAMPSHIRE

From Major (Retd) R D Jenner

1 3 November 2000

Michael A Lee
Somewhere in West Yorkshire

Dear Mr Lee,

Thank you for your letter and the offer of your services as Regimental Mascot. Should such a vacancy occur and a human selected to replace our Shetland pony you would find yourself against some stiff opposition. We would of course be obliged to advertise nationally for the post in accordance with current legislation. Naturally we would determine the terms and conditions of service. The post would be unpaid, the accommodation rudimentary and the diet agricultural. The attire would best suit someone who is accustomed to wearing leather next to the skin. As silence and steadiness on parade are prerequisites for the job there would be no requirement to dance and /or sing. With this in mind any consumption of alcohol would be out of the question.

The present incumbent has only been in post two years. He is considerably younger than you and whilst no fell-runner could probably give a good account of himself on the flat. I do not anticipate that he will be replaced in the short term. However don't give up hope and keep your eye on the "Situations Vacant" columns of the national press. Remember that these days change is the natural order of things!

Yours sincerely

Roger Jenner

Copy to : Regimental Mascot

**Major [Retd] R. D. Jenner
The Parachute Regimental Association
Browning Barracks
Aldershot GU11 2BU
Hampshire**

Dear Major Jenner

First and foremost let me thank you for an excellent reply dated 13 November 2000 to my application for the job of Regimental Mascot to the Parachute Regiment. At first I was exceedingly disappointed to hear that you not only had a perfectly adequate Shetland Pony fulfilling mascot duties for the regiment but also that this equine individual is considerably younger than myself and consequently I applied for some alternative positions I thought might be of personal interest. Of the many opportunities I sought they included 'Harbourmaster' for Wigan Pier, 'Deputy Raven-Master' at the Tower of London, and even 'The Sheriff of Nottingham'. Alas – none of these applications has borne even the smallest of fruit of potential employment and as in the case of my letter to Prince Andrew applying to be 'The Grand Old Duke of York' I have not even received a reply.

Having re-read your kind response, therefore, I have arrived at the conclusion that it is time to return to the original idea, express my belief in a competitive attitude to career aspirations and to reaffirm my initial desire for 'mascot status.' If, for whatever reason, the Shetland Pony finds himself/herself no longer capable of the requirements demanded by an elite regiment please do consider me an appropriate replacement. I am willing to accept the terms and conditions of service as you mentioned provided that I might supplement this 'unpaid post' with other part-time work, that I am assured of a roof over my 'rudimentary accommodation' and that the 'agricultural diet' includes a healthy selection of vegetables [I am not too fond of sugar beet every meal time!]. With regards to the 'wearing of leather next to the skin' I have my hesitations but have bought a good quality watchstrap as a starter. Furthermore I am willing to curtail the alcohol-induced singing and dancing as I can fully appreciate your comments around the need for silence and steadiness on parade. Perhaps I might enjoy a pint or two of off-duty Calibre and a little quiet whistling instead? Finally, despite my entering for the third time this coming Spring the Man vs Horse vs Bike Mountain Marathon in Wales and am training on the Yorkshire moors in preparation, I am also applying myself to 'giving a good account of myself on the flat' by running along a local canal towpath from time to time.

I am quite willing to challenge your Shetland Pony to a race on either terrain over a twenty miles distance. Rather than wait until the position becomes vacant and 'advertise nationally in accordance with current legislation' perhaps the winner of such a race should take all and 'win' the mascot post. As you quite rightly say 'change is certainly the natural order of things these days' and I would certainly make a noticeable change to the regimental order of things if you exchanged mascot from the wee pony with the short legs to me; the hairy-chested fell-runner from Yorkshire. Failing that would there be any chance of an honorary membership of the Parachute Regimental Association?

Yours tenaciously

Michael A. Lee

UTRINQUE PARATUS

AD UNUM OMNES

THE PARACHUTE REGIMENTAL ASSOCIATION
Patron: HIS ROYAL HIGHNESS THE PRINCE OF WALES, KG, KT, PC, GCB, AK, QSO, ADC

From Major (Retd) R D Jenner

BROWNING BARRACKS
ALDERSHOT, GU11 2BU
HAMPSHIRE

Michael A Lee
Somewhere in West Yorkshire

22 February 2001

Dear Mr Lee,

Thank you for your letter. I regret to inform you that at a recent high level regimental conference, confidence in our present mascot was confirmed unequivocally. Given his present tender age and the fact that his predecessor was not retired until well into his teens it will be some time before a vacancy occurs. I suspect that by then in spite of having run up many hills you will be well over the hill. The age of retirement for humans in the services is 55. Exceptions are made for a handful of very senior officers, but not for mascots!

I note that you have applied without success for a number of posts. Have you considered applying to one of those Welsh regiments that has a goat as mascot? With your fell running experience you have much to offer. Why not look them up after your race this spring.

A race is out of the question. For you to compete on equal terms you would have iron shoes nailed to the palms of your hands and soles of your feet. There would be no anaesthetic of course. How is your pain threshold? Quite high I imagine being a fell runner. Nevertheless at some time in the future you would doubtless want some recompense for the trauma and indignity. The bad publicity and costs would be unacceptable to us.

Sadly you do not qualify for honorary membership of the PRA.. Furthermore it is not in my power to grant it. Bribery won't work either, unless you can run to £10000 to refurbish the mascot's horsebox.

In the seventies a chap calling himself Henry Root published a couple of volumes of letters written in a similar vein to yours. They are probably out of print now, but your local library might have them. They will amuse you.

Good luck in the race.

Roger Semms

Yours sincerely

Somewhere in West Yorkshire
26 October 2000

The Mayor
The Town Hall
Wigan
Lancashire

Dear Sir

I am writing to you a most unusual letter, namely to apply for the position of Harbour Master for Wigan Pier.

Aged 40, I have spent most of my career within industry but with a long-standing interest in all things nautical and particularly in port management. I am interested now in pursuing an alternative career and would be most grateful if you could advise me of any Harbour Master positions currently available within your own world-famous port within the Wigan area.

I am a conscientious and industrious individual sporting a full naval-style beard and moustache and believe not only could I fulfil any duties allocated to me in my capacity as Harbour Master but would look the part as well. I can even sing a rousing selection of sea shanties which might be a useful motivational capability for those individuals reporting to me.

I thank you for your time and consideration in this matter and look forward to hearing from you in the very near future.

Sincerely

Michael A. Lee

LEISURE AND CULTURAL SERVICES DEPARTMENT
Director : Rodney F Hill

Our Reference	RFH/GHC/Lee/35.00
Your Reference	
Please ask for	Rodney Hill
Extension	3500
Direct Line	(01942) 828500
Date	2 November 2000

Mr M A Lee
Somewhere in West Yorkshire

Dear Mr Lee

Thank you for your letter dated 26 October 2000, which was addressed to the Mayor of Wigan.

Unfortunately, I am unable to help you. Wigan Pier is in fact based on the Leeds/Liverpool canal and, as such, does not have a harbour. Neither do I have any knowledge or expertise on the career opportunities for a Harbour Master.

I suggest that you visit your nearest and largest reference library; they should have advice on career opportunities and what training would be required to become a Harbour Master.

I hope you achieve the position you wish. In the meantime, I enclose publicity about Wigan Pier, which I hope you will visit some time in the future.

Yours sincerely

Rodney F Hill
DIRECTOR OF LEISURE & CULTURAL SERVICES

c.c.   The Mayor

Please address all communications to the Director of Leisure and Cultural Services.
Leisure and Cultural Services Department, Wigan Council,
The Indoor Sports Complex, Loire Drive, Robin Park, Wigan. WN5 0UL
Telephone: (01942) 244991 Telex: 677341 Fax: (01942) 828540
Web Site: www.wiganmbc.gov.uk E-Mail: g.clarke@wiganmbc.gov.uk

Building the future together

Somewhere in West Yorkshire
29 November 2000

Director of Marketing
Lea & Perrins Worcestershire Sauce
HP Foods Limited
Tower Road
Aston Cross
Birmingham B6 5AB

Dear Sir/Madam

I am writing to you a most unusual letter, namely to ask what opportunities there might be to become 'Lea & Perrins Worcestershire Sauce Man'.

Might I suggest that L&P Worcestershire Sauce is probably one of the most important food products within its range on the British supermarket shelves and yet, though appreciated by significant numbers of people, has so much consumer potential yet untapped. Should this potential be exploited to the full I believe that your company would benefit from increased profitability and indeed even more consumers would benefit from the enjoyment and indeed nutrition that L&P Worcestershire Sauce offers.

So, having presented my situational analysis you may well be eager to hear my proposed solution? Do you remember what the Milky Bar Kid did for the sales of white milky bar chocolate? Even now, aged 40, I can remember every word from the Milky Bar Kid's song from the 1960s and as a consequence the thought of white chocolate makes my mouth water. I eat so much of it I should be a company shareholder.

If you were to employ me as 'L&P Worcestershire Sauce Man': a reasonably fit 40-year-old, and dress me in a suitable L&P Worcestershire Sauce costume, I could be filmed doing all sorts of fitness-friendly things such as running, cycling, climbing, dancing, canoeing and so on having consumed L&P Worcestershire Sauce with my eggs for breakfast or in a delicious lunchtime sandwich and broadcast with huge success on TV and placed in magazine adverts.

L&P Worcestershire Sauce could be pigeon-holed and advertised for that adult section of the market where nutrition and fitness are becoming more and more interrelated. As probably the most interested man in L&P Worcestershire Sauce in the whole of the UK I am certainly the man for the job. Will you please consider me?! Between us we could establish an L&P Worcestershire Sauce fan club, perhaps even an Internet website for members and start a new business-focused consumer cult following.

I thank you for your time and consideration and look forward to hearing from you in the very near future.

Also in the meantime, would there be any courtesy sample bottles of L&P Worcestershire Sauce I could request in order to stock up my Christmas cupboard?

Sincerely and mouth-wateringly

M. A. Lee

Michael A. Lee

HP Foods Limited

HP Foods Limited, Tower Road, Aston Cross, Birmingham, B6 5AB
Tel : 0121 - 359 4911 : Fax : 0121 - 380 2335

Please reply to :-

Our Ref: 4449

01 December 2000

Mr Lee
Somewhere in West Yorkshire

Dear Mr Lee

Re: L&P Worcestershire Sauce

Thank you for your recent letter and your compliments on our L&P Worcestershire Sauce. We are extremely pleased that you find our product so versatile and economical.

We enclose a product voucher so that you may sample and enjoy some of the other products in our range and have passed your interesting offer to our marketing department for their consideration!

It is always pleasant to receive comments and opinions from valued customers, such as yourself, and we thank you for taking the time to write. These comments help us to assess the market and our consumers which hopefully helps us to meet their demands.

We hope that you continue to enjoy our products in the future.

Yours sincerely

Caroline Saunders
Consumer Services

Registered Office: Mollison Avenue, Enfield, Middlesex EN3 7JZ.
Telephone: (44) 0990 326663 Facsimile: (44) 0990 134881
Registered in England No. 2251694

A **DANONE** GROUP COMPANY

Somewhere in West Yorkshire
7 December 2000

**The Manager
John Lewis
Oxford Street
London W1A 1EX**

Dear Sir/Madam

I am writing to you a most unusual letter, namely to apply for the position of 'The Rather Jolly Mobile Christmas Tree' at the John Lewis Department Store of Oxford Street. I guess that it is fair to say that although the idea of a Christmas Grotto complete with Santa Claus is a well established and popular tradition in many department stores that of a 'Rather Jolly Mobile Christmas Tree' is probably a novel one. So, here is the idea in detail.

If you were to employ me as the aforementioned Christmas tree dressed appropriately in coniferous foliage and decorated with a range of suitable baubles and lights I could spend my time planting myself at various key locations within the store to greet the customers in a festive and hearty manner. Every now and then I could uproot myself and wander off in as tree-like manner as possible to the next location and repeat the whole process to the delight of your many customers. The benefits I am sure would include the drawing of curious individuals into your store swelling the ranks of potential shoppers, raising the Christmas spirit in a way conducive to relaxed spending and indeed increasing even further the profitability for your business as a result. In addition I could keep an arboreal eye open for the odd dastardly shoplifter and wrap my branches around that person whilst security was summoned.

I believe it is 'fir' to say that once 'spruced' up I would offer an interesting and mood elevating attraction and dare I say it am 'pineing' to hear from you reference my application. I trust that you have not had a 'forest' of similar letters and consequently will still be able to see the 'wood from the trees'. Many thanks for your time and consideration and I look forward to hearing from you in the very near future. In the meantime should you feel that my letter deserves an acknowledgement in the form of a small hamper of delicious John Lewis food, if indeed you have hampers of this kind, I am sure that my family saplings and I would do enormous justice to its' mouth-watering consumption.

Sincerely, with seasons greetings and ever the Yorkshire Opportunist,

Michael A. Lee

JOHN LEWIS
Oxford Street

18 December 2000
REC/JEB/31

A branch of the
John Lewis Partnership

Oxford Street
London W1A 1EX
Telephone (020) 7629 7711

Direct Line 0171 514 5337

<u>Personal</u>
Mr M A Lee

Somewhere in West Yorkshire

Dear Mr Lee

Thank you for your recent letter enquiring about possible employment with John Lewis.

I regret to inform you that we have no suitable vacancies at present, and are, therefore, unable to consider your application. We are rather concerned that you would have to 'uproot' yourself from Huddersfield but if you would like to contact any of our other 'branches', we would of course 'leaf' that decision to 'yew'.

I would like to mention however that I very much enjoyed reading your letter and I would like to wish you a very happy Christmas.

I am sorry I cannot be of more help, but would like to thank you for the interest you have shown.

Yours sincerely

Mrs J E Britton
Staff Office

CALEYS
Windsor

A branch of the
John Lewis Partnership

High Street
Windsor
Berkshire SL4 1LL
Telephone (01753) 863241

FIH/CW
29 December 2000

Mr Michael A Lee
Somewhere in West Yorkshire

Dear Mr Lee,

Thank you for your letter of 7 December 2000 which has been forwarded to us by one of our other 'branches'.

After 'conifering' with other members of management, I believe that the option of a jolly mobile Christmas tree is not viable for Caleys and this 'leaves' me no choice but to decline your kind offer.

May I wish you and yours a happy and prosperous New Year.

Yours sincerely,

Frances Hickman
General Manager

Somewhere in West Yorkshire
19 December 2000

The Commanding Officer
Marine Nationale
2, Rue Royale
PARIS 8
00350 Armees
France

Dear Sir

I am writing to you a most unusual letter, namely to ask what opportunities are available to me in securing a job with the French Navy as a 'Submarine Periscope Polishing Executive'.

I have for many years been fascinated by the concept of travel beneath the ocean and particularly by the notion of observing objects which are above the surface of the water through the periscope of a suitably submerged submarine. It concerns me to think that should the eyepiece of a periscope be dusty or greasy, appropriate military observation could be severely compromised and, of course, in a critical battle situation could mean the difference between victory and defeat.

If you were to employ me as a 'Submarine Periscope Polishing Executive' I would endeavour to ensure all my periscopes were as clean as clean can be and 100 per cent operational all of the time. I am a jolly good polisher at the best of times and should you require references my wife has agreed to supply them on request. She has also asked whether I might be assigned to a submarine that spends a considerable time away from port and is often deep under the ocean far from land.

In addition she felt a French naval training programme would be an interesting contrast to my present work in the UK and although she knows we would not see each other as often as we do at present, thought it a potentially enriching and horizon – widening experience. I am not wholly sure why this would be her wish but I respect her greatly.

Many thanks for your time and consideration and I look forward to hearing from you in the very near future.

Sincerely

Michael A. Lee

PS I am most willing to learn to speak French.

MINISTÈRE DE LA DÉFENSE

Paris, le **.15 JAN. 2001**

N° 86 SIRPA/Marine/NP

**MARINE
NATIONALE**

SERVICE D'INFORMATION
ET DE RELATIONS PUBLIQUES
DE LA MARINE
2, RUE ROYALE · PARIS 8ᵉ
00350 ARMÉES
TÉLÉPHONE 01 42 92 16 39 (MARINE 21 639)
FAX 01 40 20 04 90

Sir Michael A. Lee
Somewhere in West Yorkshire

Dear Sir,

I have been very interested in your proposition of becoming the french navy first 'submarine periscope polishing executive'. The inconvenience of our dusty and greasy periscopes has been thouroughly and extensively analysed by the international press (La Dépêche de Montauvert 10.01.2000, The Times 30.02.2000, The Longwood Chronicle 07.05.2000).

Moreover, your private and wise initiative reinforces the close military cooperation between our two countries.
I suggest a slight extension to your proposition in order to cover both our submarine and outerspace activities. Spy satellites also require clean glasses. By the way, the human physical requirements to rotate around the planet, attached to a satellite are close to those required for operational deep sea periscope polishing.

May I propose that we meet to examine the details related to your future employment of 'submarine periscope & spy satellite glasses polishing executive'. A convenient place for me would be on the top of the mid-Atlantic ridge (depth minus 1054 meters) by 40°N in two weeks. Just knock at the door of my greasy periscope.

Sincerely.

Capitaine de vaisseau Olivier Lajous

**The Director General
MI5**

Dear Sir/Madam

I am writing to you a most unusual letter, namely to suggest to you that I might have been approached in a rather clever but round-about fashion to become a French spy and thought it best to air my concerns to yourself or indeed MI6 if more appropriate.

Shortly before Xmas 2000 I wrote a spoof job application to the Commanding Officers of various world navies asking to be employed as a 'Submarine Periscope Polishing Executive' in a bid to receive some interesting replies for a book I am writing. [I attach a copy of the letter sent to the French Navy]

To my great delight and indeed amusement I received an excellent reply from a Captain in the French Ministry of Defence embracing my job idea with significant enthusiasm and indeed encouraging some extended duties to include cleaning the glasses on the French Spy satellites. He also suggested we met to discuss the idea further as you will read in a copy of his reply as enclosed.

Now call me old fashioned if you will but does this not appear to be a classic spy recruitment scenario? It has all the elements of foreign surveillance strategy; calling me 'Sir' to create rapport and goodwill hence buttering me up for the recruitment process, a mention of space-based spy satellites, and indeed a suggestion of a covert meeting in a far less than visible place where secretive liaison could take place. What's more Captain Lajous has suggested that my employment might 'reinforce close military co-operation between our two countries.' The whole thing makes my spine tingle!

I can assure you that I am a loyal and patriotic citizen of the UK, a born and bred Yorkshireman, and in no way inclined to spy for the French but would be most interested to hear from you with any words of advice you might have for me. Should there be any need for me to write to MI6 separately or indeed send a copy of my concerns to any MI6-employed personnel with an interest in recruitment matters, please do let me know.

Sincerely

Michael A. Lee

PO BOX 3255
LONDON
SW1P 1AE

Mr M Lee   7 March 2001
Somewhere in West Yorkshire

Dear Mr Lee

Thank you for your letter of 14 February 2001.

It would appear that the reply you received from the French Ministry of Defence is nothing more than a humorous response to your spoof application.

Yours sincerely,

The Director General

Somewhere in West Yorkshire
21 December 2000

The Duke of Edinburgh
Buckingham Palace
London

Dear Sir

I am writing to you a most unusual letter, namely to apply for the position of 'Gentleman Usher of the Black Rod' at the House of Lords.

Aged 41, I have almost twenty years' experience working within an industry which depends greatly on communication skills and as a consequence have developed a strong, clear voice should I be required to announce my presence to those of the Commons in any verbal manner. More importantly I have had substantial experience beating on my own front door when returning from the local public house late in the evening in an attempt to persuade my disgruntled wife to release the door-bolts and let me in and this I have done on many occasions. Usually she has agreed to an admission!

Although I have not undertaken this 'summoning' with an ebony stick surmounted with a gold lion – as I would with my staff of office should I be successful in my application for the job – I have brandished various large sticks that have fallen from oak, ash and beech trees in my back garden and knocked heartily in a way that has helped me significantly refine my knocking skills.

If I was employed for the aforementioned job and became a personal attendant of the Sovereign, I can assure you that I am a Royalist and wholeheartedly support our Royal traditions and ceremonies.

I do hope that you will consider me for the job and look forward to hearing from you in the very near future.

Sincerely

M. A. Lee

Michael A. Lee

From: Captain Jamie Lyon, Grenadier Guards

BUCKINGHAM PALACE

9th January, 2001.

Dear Mr Lee,

    The Duke of Edinburgh has asked me to thank you for your letter, the contents of which have been noted.

Yours sincerely

[signature]

Temporary Equerry

Mr. Michael A. Lee

BUCKINGHAM PALACE, LONDON. SW1A 1AA

Somewhere in West Yorkshire
1 January 2001

The Chief Executive
The Guildhall
Nottingham NG1 4BT

Dear Sir/Madam

I am writing to you a most unusual letter, namely to ask whether there still exists the position 'Sheriff of Nottingham' and if so, if I might apply for the position when it next becomes available.

Ever since I was a small boy I have had an interest in the ancient stories of Robin Hood and his merry men, of Sherwood Forest, and in the swashbuckling adventures of all concerned. It strikes me however that stealing from anyone, whether rich or poor, is not exactly the most civilised way of going about the pursuit of justice and has led me to believe that the historical Sheriff of Nottingham was probably not quite the scoundrel he was made out to be. If in 2001 a band of sword-wielding, forest-dwelling rascals came around to my house, threatened my family and I and stole our computer, I would be most aggrieved and keen to seek the help of the local police.

Should therefore a position be available for me to apply to become the current Sheriff of Nottingham I believe I would be a worthy candidate for several reasons; I am an honest, hardworking member of the community. I like Nottingham and, should the need arise, could travel there easily from West Yorkshire by car or train. I once rode a horse in Canada and so could pose for the press when required although I guess it is fair to say that a motor vehicle of some description would be more suitable these days. Should any modern day criminals take refuge in local woods I am an experienced orienteer and fell runner and would almost certainly track them down. Finally, I love banqueting and would relish the chance to dine at Nottingham Castle.

I thank you for your time and consideration and look forward to hearing from you in the very near future. May I also wish you a very happy New Year.

Sincerely

Michael A. Lee

Corporate Affairs

Chief Executive's Department
The Guildhall
Nottingham
NG1 4BT
Tel: 0115 915 4725
Fax: 0115 915 4434
~~email: julia.gunn@nottinghamcity.gov.uk~~
Email: chris.bowron@nottinghamcity.gov.uk

Mr Michael Lee
Somewhere in West Yorkshire

15 January 2001

Dear Mr Lee

Thank you for your letter dated 1st January 2001, in which you state your desire to be considered for the role of Sheriff of Nottingham.

It is traditional that the following requirements should be met before assuming this role:

- You must be elected as a councillor to represent a ward of Nottingham

- You are nominated by your fellow councillors to be elected as the Sheriff of Nottingham.

I hope that this information is useful to you.

Nottingham City Council would like to thank you for showing a great interest in our city and would like you to accept the enclosed gift as a token of our appreciation. *

Yours sincerely

Chris Bowron
Service Manager
Corporate Promotions

(*This was a tie embroidered with the Nottingham heraldic crest.)

Nottingham
our style is legendary

Printed on recycled paper

Chief Executive
ABTA
68–71 Newman Street
London W1P 4AH

Dear Sir

I am writing to you a most unusual letter, namely to ask if you might help me find a rather different holiday based on a travel book I read recently involving journeys to several remote parts of the world and therefore become a 'Holidaymaker with a Difference'. Whether it would be possible to visit all of the places mentioned in the travel book over a single extended holiday or whether I would have to plan the complete package of journeys over a series of holidays I am not sure, but would be most grateful for your help either way.

I understand that the journey between many of the island destinations described by the author was by boat but I am unable to pinpoint the exact location of some of these islands in my world atlas. I do, however, have in front of me a list of place-names which might be of help and are as follows: Brobdingnag, Laputa, Balnibarbi, and Luggnagg. I believe that there was a visit to 'the country of the Houyhnhnms' also.

I was extremely interested to read the descriptions of these places in the aforementioned travel book which, incidentally was written by a Mr J Swift, and must admit that my imagination and desire to visit them has been significantly stimulated. The thoughts of wading through fields of giant corn beneath a blue sky, warm sun and close to the sea is most appealing when considered in the midst of an English Winter. I was not particularly excited by the prospect of meeting pirates as was the case in one of the travel books' chapters but thought that since there is significantly more security in international waters than was the case when the book was written this would not be a real modern-day threat.

I do hope that you will be able to assist me in my search for a holiday which involves some or all of the places I have mentioned and would be grateful for advice around holiday costings, recommended times to travel and other relevant information, such as required vaccinations, and look forward to hearing from you in the very near future.

Many thanks for your time and consideration.

Sincerely

Michael A. Lee

68-71 Newman Street
London W1P 4AH
Telephone: 020 7637 2444
Telefax: 020 7637 0713
Email: abta@abta.co.uk

ABTA

The Association of British Travel Agents Ltd
Registered in England No 551311 London

Mr. M.A. Lee,

Somewhere in West Yorkshire

ITR/JDA/3566

11 January, 2001

Dear Mr. Lee,

Thank you for your letter, 9 January 2001, from which I was interested to learn of your planned journey.

I fear that it may be inadvisable to visit the islands you have identified, as I understand the natives may be hostile particularly the extremely large citizens of Brobdingnag and the rather superior horse-like inhabitants of Houyhnhnms. Accordingly, the Foreign and Commonwealth Office have consistently issued advice not to visit these destinations except in your dreams.

With regards to our advice as to whether it would be best to make a single extended trip or a series of individual holidays, I would caution that unless you can assemble an extremely large group of children with powerful lungs you currently lack the propulsion available to Mr. Gulliver when making his voyage, and therefore may find it difficult to reach your intended destination in either case.

I am sorry to send you such a disappointing reply but hope you will not be deterred from making alternative holiday arrangements this year with one of our members.

Yours sincerely,

I.T. REYNOLDS
CHIEF EXECUTIVE

INVESTOR IN PEOPLE

Select World Travel

31 Haven Road . Canford Cliffs . Poole . Dorset . BH13 7LE . United Kingdom

Telephone: Bournemouth 01202 709881 • Fax: 01202 707662

E-mail: info@selectworldtravel.co.uk • Web: www.selecttravel.co.uk

10 January 2000   RR/MAL

Mr Michael Lee
Somewhere in West Yorkshire

Dear Mr. Lee,

Thank you for your letter of 9th January requesting help in arranging a somewhat different type of holiday.

The book that you refer to as having recently read must, I think, be "Gulliver's Travels" and I regret to advise you that it is in fact a work of fiction and none of the places you mention actually exist.

I have to admit that on first reading your letter it occurred to me that maybe it was a "wind up", if you will excuse the expression. But, on reflection it occurred to me that perhaps the writer, having become disillusioned with the service offered by most travel agents, had hit upon an unusual way of sorting the wheat from the chaff.

At Select World Travel we do pride ourselves on finding the right holiday for even the most exacting of clients – and am sure we could assist you in finding that very unusual holiday.

If you would like to pursue the matter further, please do not hesitate to call me so that we may discuss your requirements.

Yours sincerely,

Robert Readman
Manager.

    Select World Travel is a division of Select Worldchoice Limited
Registered Office: 1 St. Stephen's Court, St. Stephen's Road, Bournemouth BH2 6LA
Registered in England Number: 3514295 VAT Registration Number: 717 5498 05   worldchoice

Somewhere in West Yorkshire
13 March 2001

Mr R. Readman
Manager
Select World Travel
31 Haven Road
Canford Cliffs
Poole BH13 7LE
Dorset

Dear Mr Readman

First and foremost I would like to thank you for your letter of the 10th January concerning my enquiry around visiting the Islands of Laputa, Brobdingnag, Balnibarbi, Luggnagg and the 'country of the Houyhnhnms'.

I am grateful to you for pointing out to me that these islands do not actually exist other than in the mind of the writer Jonathan Swift and learning that his was a work of fiction 'Gulliver's Travels' and not a travel book as such has certainly helped explain why I could not find them in my world atlas. It is also clear now why some of the descriptions concerning rather small people and giants appeared to be so exaggerated!

As far as priding yourselves at Select World Travel at 'finding the right holiday for even the most exacting of clients' I am indeed sure that you might be able to assist me further and find for me an 'that very unusual holiday' alternative to my previous request especially in the light of my obvious and recent disappointment.

In this regard I would be most interested to know if you could offer suggestions regards my enjoying an activity holiday this coming summer which would, I suggest, offer an enormous amount of fun and indeed add a significant element of education also.

Very recently I was reading a well-thumbed copy of a book by a certain Mr Archy O'Logy; an Irish writer I presume, who described a place famous for its' fossils and ancient history called Gondwanaland. I have not had a great deal of time over the last few weeks to research this place or indeed to look at holiday options as my workload has been particularly heavy and so would be most obliged if you could help me in finding a package that would include travel to and from Gondwanaland, accommodation and including potential for some fossil-hunting excursions.

I would also be grateful for any information around currency required in Gondwanaland and any well-written and informative travel-guides that you might recommend. I have already bought myself a new magnifying glass and pith helmet and am really looking forward to firming up a holiday booking and setting out on a refreshing and exciting summer vacation.

Many thanks indeed for your time and consideration and I appreciate the interest you have shown in finding for me that 'very unusual holiday alternative'.

Sincerely

M. A. Lee

Michael A. Lee

Select World Travel

31 Haven Road . Canford Cliffs . Poole . Dorset . BH13 7LE . United Kingdom

Telephone: Bournemouth 01202 709881 • Fax: 01202 707662

E-mail: info@selectworldtravel.co.uk • Web: www.selecttravel.co.uk

21 March 2001

Mr Michael A. Lee
Somewhere in West Yorkshire

Dear Mr. Lee,

I am in receipt of your letter dated 13th March regarding the possibility of a holiday in Gondwanaland.

However, I fear that once again I must disillusion you. Gondwanaland does not in fact exist. Gondwanaland or Gondwana are the names given to a hypothetical supercontinent in the Southern Hemisphere which comprised the land masses that now make up Africa, Australia, India and South America some 200 million years ago.

So, while Gondwanaland itself does not in fact exist, it would be possible to visit the continents which at one time supposedly formed it. Probably the best way of doing so would be to take advantage of one of a number of extremely good value Round-the-World fares that are available these days. One of the best being the Star Alliance fare of £1399.00 for Economy travel and £3199.00 for Business Class travel. These fares are valid for 1 year of travel, allow a minimum of 3 stops and a maximum of 15, with a maximum permitted mileage of 29,000 miles. This fare does not include airport taxes.

If you care to let me know which places your are interested in visiting I will be happy to work on a provisional itinerary for you.

We do require a non-refundable payment of £25.00 to be paid before we undertake involved, tailor-made enquires. This payment would however, become part of your payment should you decide to go ahead with the booking.

I look forward to assisting you with your travel arrangements.

Sincere regards,

Robert Readman, Manager.

   Select World Travel is a division of Select Worldchoice Limited
Registered Office: 1 St. Stephen's Court, St. Stephen's Road, Bournemouth BH2 6LA
Registered in England Number: 3514295 VAT Registration Number: 717 5498 05   worldchoice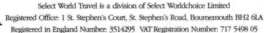

Mr R. Readman
Manager
Select World Travel
31 Haven Road
Canford Cliffs
Poole BH13 7LE
Dorset

Dear Mr Readman

First and foremost I would like to thank you for your letter dated 21 March 2001 concerning my enquiry around visiting Gondwanaland.

I am most grateful to you for pointing out that once again my interest has been misplaced in a region that doesn't actually exist; or at least has not existed for many years if ever at all. I intend to revisit the book that described this non-existent land and perhaps even write to the author; a certain Archy O'Logy, and complain about the misinformation supplied therein.

I also thank you for taking the time and effort to write to me about ways in which I might visit many of the continents that were thought at one time to form Gondwanaland. This information has been most helpful.

However, having already been disappointed on two occasions as a direct consequence of reading what I believed were authoritative travel books, I have decided to obtain some ideas for my summer holiday from personal recommendations instead. In this regard, I would be most grateful for any advice you might have for me reference a holiday destination of significant interest.

Only last week I met an old friend of mine in the local doctors surgery waiting room who explained that he had, a little while ago, been feeling significantly below par and in need of a holiday. He had felt constantly tired, somewhat depressed and was gaining weight. Having spoken to his GP I gather he found the solution to his problems in what I presume to be a group of islands called the Islets of Langerhans.

My friend described the degree of contrast he had experienced after hearing about the Islets of Langerhans and told me that not only was he refreshed and back to normal weight but that even his great thirst had been quenched. I have never seen a man so changed by a holiday!

Once again I have been scouring my world atlas but cannot find this group of islands anywhere. I presume that the word 'Islets' suggest a relatively small landmass and so would require a more experienced search than is possible with my own reference source. Mr Readman, if you were able to help me in my quest for this destination I am sure I will have found the answer to my 2001 holiday needs. Incidentally, I seem to remember my friend mentioning something about travelling there by Pan Creas Airlines or Shipping; I wonder if that might be of help in your research.

… continued

Once again many thanks indeed for your time and consideration and I look forward to hearing from you in the very near future.

Sincerely

Michael A. Lee

Select World Travel

31 Haven Road . Canford Cliffs . Poole . Dorset . BH13 7LE . United Kingdom

Telephone: Bournemouth 01202 709881 • Fax: 01202 707662

E-mail: info@selectworldtravel.co.uk • Web: www.selecttravel.co.uk

09 April 2001   RR/MAL

Mr Michael A. Lee
Somewhere in West Yorkshire

Dear Mr Lee,

I am in receipt of your latest letter regarding your ongoing quest for that 'rather different holiday' in which you express an interest in visiting the Islets of Langerhans.

However, I fear that yet again you have been misled.

I do not know if you ever saw a film entitled "The Incredible Journey", in which a researcher was shrunk to a microscopic size, placed in an equally microscopic submarine and injected into the vein of a another person and then proceeded to explore that person's body?

This, I am afraid, is the only way in which you could ever visit the Islets of Langerhans as they are located on one's pancreas – and are named after the doctor who discovered them.

As a matter of interest, "Where are the Islets of Langerhans?" is a trick question often included in travel quizzes.   And I seem to recall that the same question is also included in the game of "Trivial Pursuit".

I am sorry to have to disappoint you once again, but I suspect that the friend you met at your doctor's surgery thoroughly enjoyed pulling your leg!

For myself, I am intrigued wondering just where this is all leading.

Sincere regards,

Robert Readman
Manager.

Select World Travel is a division of Select Worldchoice Limited
Registered Office: 1 St. Stephen's Court, St. Stephen's Road, Bournemouth BH2 6LA
Registered in England Number: 3514295 VAT Registration Number: 717 5498 05

Somewhere in West Yorkshire
17 April 2001

Mr R. Readman
Manager
Select World Travel
31 Haven Road
Canford Cliffs
Poole BH13 7LE
Dorset

Dear Mr Readman

First and foremost I would like to thank you for your letter dated 9 April 2001 in reply
to my enquiries around visiting the Islets of Langerhans. I am grateful to you for explaining to
me that these 'islets' are not small islands as I first thought but rather specialised organs
located on the pancreas and, as I have since discovered, apparently responsible for secreting
the hormone insulin.

When I realised that yet again my search for an interesting and restful holiday had
been misdirected I contacted the old friend I had met in the doctors surgery and asked
him why he had so cruelly led me up the garden path. I am a little embarrassed to tell you that
the fault was not his; alas it was confusion in my own understanding of what he was telling
me. This unfortunate fellow had indeed felt constantly tired, somewhat depressed and was
gaining weight but the focus mentioned to him around the Islets of Langerhans by his
GP was in reference to his development of Type 2 Diabetes and his apparent
refreshment to the initiation of appropriate medical treatment. I cannot believe I
misunderstood his tale to the degree that I would apply for a 'similar holiday' as a result!

On the subject of medical matters I am amazed to read in your recent letter that
modern technology has now enabled 'a researcher to be shrunk to a microscopic size,
placed in an equally microscopic submarine and injected into the vein of another person'
and moreover that a film has been made of this. This documentary surely deserves the title *The
Incredible Journey* and I will certainly look out for it on my Cable TV Discovery channel. It
sounds truly amazing.

Do you think there will be any commercial applications as far as this technological
advance is concerned in the context of holiday excursions? If there were I would, within certain
price constraints, be most interested in being shrunk to the same size as the aforementioned
researcher and submarine and be injected into the bodies of various notable individuals. It may
be quite revealing to explore the unknown cerebral depths of grey matter belonging to various
British politicians or indeed the workings of the ears of certain rap musicians.

… continued

For pure relaxation, however, I think I would have to choose, if in agreement, the bodies of various supermodels simply to marvel at their construction and general fitness.
I would be most interested to know if there is anything currently available in this regard or whether this would be something to consider at some point in the future. Finally, Mr Readman, as far as your intrigue is concerned as to where 'all this is leading' I would say simply that I am looking for 'that very unusual holiday' to make 2001 a year to remember and relish and to achieve my ambition of becoming a 'Holidaymaker with a difference'.

Many thanks again for your time and consideration and I look forward to hearing from you in the very near future.

Sincerely

Michael A. Lee

Select World Travel

31 Haven Road . Canford Cliffs . Poole . Dorset . BH13 7LE . United Kingdom
Telephone: Bournemouth 01202 709881 • Fax: 01202 707662
E-mail: info@selectworldtravel.co.uk • Web: www.selecttravel.co.uk

03 May 2001   RR/MAL

Mr Michael A. Lee
Somewhere in West Yorkshire

Dear Mr. Lee,

My apologies for the delay in replying to your letter of 17th April, but I have been away on vacation.

I am pleased to forward four brochures that I feel may offer suggestions for that rather special holiday you are looking for.

I have included the Tauck World Discovery Antarctica brochure – although it is for the period January/February 2002 (the Antarctic Summer).

Australia, of course, offers unbounded possibilities for the adventurous, But I have included the Australasia By Rail brochure as I do feel that train travel is one of the best ways to see a country.

Costa Rica has not yet been spoilt by mass tourism and is one of the most eco-friendly nations in the world.

I do hope that you may find something in these brochures that stimulates your interest.

Once you have had a chance to study them, please do not hesitate to call if you have any questions or would like further information on a particular holiday or destination.

Sincere regards,

Robert Readman
Manager.

      Select World Travel is a division of Select Worldchoice Limited
Registered Office: 1 St. Stephen's Court, St. Stephen's Road, Bournemouth BH2 6LA
Registered in England Number: 3514295   VAT Registration Number: 717 5498 05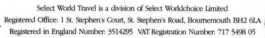

Somewhere in West Yorkshire
25 February 2001

Head of Personnel
North Cornwall District Council
Higher Trenant Road
Wadebridge
Cornwall PL27 6TW

Dear Sir

I am writing to you a most unusual letter, namely to apply for the position of 'Beast of Bodmin Moor' if indeed this position is currently available.

I would be most grateful for your advice on this matter but it does seem to me as though a significant time period has passed since any news of the so-called 'Beast of Bodmin Moor' appeared in the media and I can't help wondering whether the incumbent of past years has disappeared from the scene through retirement, career change or as the quarry of a successful hunter.

Aged 41, I am presently employed within industry as a sales executive but am keen to pursue alternative opportunities that might offer some new interest, challenge and indeed variety to life. I believe I would be an ideal candidate for the position of 'Beast of Bodmin Moor' since I have a great love of the great outdoors and am, as I believe was the previous 'Beast', a very hairy individual. I am well known for my roaring and howling and am as happy sleeping in a wooded copse or cave as I am in my own bed at home. In addition, I am rather fond of lamb-chops and though I generally buy mine at a supermarket or restaurant I would certainly consider a more natural supply if this would help the cause of the 'Beast of Bodmin Moor' legend to continue in a vigorous fashion.

As a member of the Fell Runners Association I am in excellent physical condition and experienced in the navigation of and survival in challenging terrain and well able to keep ahead of the majority of potential trackers.

I would not expect a particularly high salary although I would be most interested to know if, as part and parcel of the job package, there would be the funding for a new pair of Walsh fell-running shoes and some equipment with which to create panther tracks. An assorted bag of big-cat teeth would also be helpful.

I thank you for your time and consideration and look forward to hearing from you in the very near future.

Yours sincerely

Michael A. Lee

NORTH CORNWALL DISTRICT COUNCIL

finance &
administration

Mr. M.A. Lee
Somewhere in West Yorkshire

Higher Trenant Road
Wadebridge
Cornwall
PL27 6TW

Telephone
01208 893231

Fax
01208 893232

Email

Please ask for
Mr C C Burnham

Your Ref

My Ref
CCB/JMS

6 March 2001

H Chapman CPFA IRRV
Director of Finance &
Administration

Dear Mr. Lee

Beast of Bodmin Moor

Thank you for your letter applying for the above position.

Despite qualities and characteristics which would seem admirably to suit you for this role, as detailed in your letter, regrettably I have to inform you that, owing to financial constraints, the Council is having to withdraw its support for this post at the end of the current contract.

The present postholder, who is on a seasonal "as and when" contract, has had his hours of work steadily reduced over the past few years, to the point where they are, quite frankly, a mere remnant of their former heyday and some elements of the community are beginning to ask "what's the point?"

This is all very disappointing for us in the Personnel Department, who see the Beast as one or our more enterprising Staff Development initiatives. You may like to know that, like yourself, for years the current Beast, Ebeneezer Peabody, occupied a Senior Management position, but following a stringent selection procedure, including psychometric testing, he embarked on a specially tailored "deconstruction programme", whereby he was systematically stripped of the goal-orientated, focused behaviour which had dampened his spirits and held back the development of his inner aura for so long. In parallel, his perverse leanings towards leadership qualities, performance management and teamwork and his predilection for phrases culled from the latest management textbooks were successfully reduced to a sequence of pre-cultural pounces, jumps, yelps and grunts. However, as you may imagine, this was a very resource-intensive operation, which in the current economic climate we cannot afford to repeat.

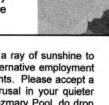

I am grateful for your interest in applying for the post and for bringing a ray of sunshine to these rather gloomy winter days. I wish you well in your search for alternative employment and am certain that in time you will find a niche to suit your evident talents. Please accept a copy of the 2001 North Cornwall Guide with my compliments for perusal in your quieter moments and of course, if you are ever down here in the vicinity of Dozmary Pool, do drop in.

Yours sincerely

Chris Burnham

Head of Personnel

THE BEST OF BODMIN MOOR
MARKETING GROUP

Hon. Secretary: Colliford Tavern
St Neot
Liskeard
Cornwall
PL14 6PZ

Tel: 01208 821335

8th May 2001

Mr M A Lee
Somewhere in West Yorkshire

Dear Mr Lee

With reference to your letter of 25th February 2001, which has been referred to our group. Firstly, thank you for your excellent application for the position of 'Beast of Bodmin Moor'. The present incumbent may well wish to stand down for a time, as the rigours of public notoriety and endeavours to avoid the papparrazi are becoming a strain on his family life.

If you will kindly forward your curriculum vitae, references and a recent photograph, we will be pleased to give your application further consideration.

Yours sincerely

Laura Edwards

Laura Edwards (Miss)
Hon. Secretary
The Best of Bodmin Moor Marketing Group

Somewhere in West Yorkshire
8 March 2001

Mr C. Burnham
Head of Personnel
North Cornwall District Council
Higher Trenant Road
Wadebridge PL27 6TW
Cornwall

Dear Mr Burnham

Many thanks indeed for your excellent reply with reference to my application to become the next 'Beast of Bodmin Moor'.

I was understandably disappointed to hear that financial constraints within the council are such that this position is no longer sustainable but can sympathise with such resourcing challenges.

It sounds as though the 'deconstruction process' in which your current Beast, Mr Peabody, was involved was an interesting and indeed arduous one and that his consequent development of a 'sequence of pre-cultural pounces, jumps, yelps and grunts' have made him a fitting role-model for his adventures on Bodmin Moor. He sounds to me as someone who might well have replaced the character 'Father Jack' in that memorable TV series *Father Ted* had there been such a need and should Mr Peabody have been seeking an alternative job. Here in Yorkshire I currently work with several people who make similar yelps and grunts but who sadly have never actually been deconstructed as such. Neither are they able to pounce or jump very quickly at all! They are beasts of a sort but would not survive the moors for long.

Many thanks also for your kind invitation to 'drop in' when in the vicinity of Dozmary Pool. Having looked at the 2001 North Cornwall Guide that you kindly sent me I have decided to do just that. I am currently packing my swimming trunks and making some plans to travel southwards. In the meantime I wondered if I might be so bold as to apply for the position of Sir Bedivere the Second. I assume that the original Sir Bedivere would have passed away many years ago and that his demise has left a rather important role when it comes to the casting of swords.

As a member of the Fell Runners Association I can assure you that I am reasonably strong and believe I would be an exceptionally good sword-caster. I would also be most pleased to entertain the immortal Lady of the Lake if this was part and parcel of the job description.

I trust that the ghost of Jan Tregeagle has not managed to empty the pool with his limpet shell by the time this letter reaches you, thus making the responsibilities of Sir Bedivere obsolete, and I look forward to hearing from you in the very near future.

Yours sincerely and hoping soon to be knighted

Michael A. Lee

NORTH CORNWALL DISTRICT COUNCIL

finance &
administration

Mr M A Lee
Somewhere in West Yorkshire

Higher Trenant Road
Wadebridge
Cornwall
PL27 6TW

Telephone
01208 893231

Fax
01208 893232

Email
chris.burnham@ncdc.gov.
uk

Please ask for
Chris Burnham

Dear Mr Lee

Thank you for your letter of 8th March 2001.

I note your continued interest in working for the Council in some capacity and your inventive suggestion of assuming the role of Sir Bedivere the Second.

Your Ref

I am afraid that with your limited experience of swordsmanship you would not be cut out for this sort of work. I am concerned too at your reference to 'entertaining' the Lady of the Lake; the Council simply cannot afford any bad publicity as a result of a harassment case.

My Ref
CCB/SS

16 March 2001

I am sorry to be the bearer of bad news but if you are dissatisfied may I suggest you take up your complaint with the Swordcasting Standards Council.

H Chapman CPFA IRRV
Director of Finance &
Administration

Yours sincerely

Chris Burnham

Head of Personnel

Somewhere in West Yorkshire
31 March 2001

Himself The Pope
Vatican City
Rome
Italy

Dear Sir,

I am writing to you a most unusual letter, namely to apply for the position of Quasi Modo the Second, the New Hunchback of Notre Dame Cathedral.

Presently residing in the North of England I am a mature 41-year-old man with facial features that are suitably weathered and full of character. One might say that I have an angular and rugged appearance with a slightly twisted nose and countless craggy lines upon my forehead and at the sides of my piercing eyes. I am unusual in the extent and thickness of my ginger-brown body hair and have a rug-like preponderance of the above across my chest, back and arms. If ever there was a case to be made for a possible link between the orang-utan and man, I would be a notable example. In summary, with the exception of the hump, I would be the ideal candidate to fill the role of Quasi Modo the Second, the New Hunchback of Notre Dame, on the basis that I have many of the notable physical characteristics that have come to be associated with the original resident of your fine cathedral.

In addition to the above I must tell you that as a long-standing member of the Fell Runners Association in England I am a considerably fit individual and would find it relatively easy to run up and down the cathedral steps to and from the bell tower where I assume I would be provided with suitable lodging. I have a great love of church music and would be most grateful for the opportunity to ring the bells of Notre Dame to the highest standard for the people of Paris and for France. I would also be happy to ensure the bells are cleaned and polished and kept in good condition at all times.

I would add that although I do not have a hump on my back, I would be only too pleased to wear an artificial substitute if this is a necessity of the job. I would also be willing to learn to speak French and Latin.

Many thanks indeed for your time and consideration and I look forward to hearing from you in the very near future.

Sincerely

M. A. Lee

Michael A. Lee

SECRETARIAT OF STATE

FIRST SECTION - GENERAL AFFAIRS

From the Vatican, 15 May 2001

Dear Mr Lee,

His Holiness Pope John Paul II duly received your letter and has directed me to reply in his name.

His Holiness appreciates the sentiments which prompted you to write and he will remember you in his prayers.

Yours sincerely,

Monsignor Pédro López Quintana
Assessor

Mr Michael A. Lee
Somewhere in West Yorkshire

Somewhere in West Yorkshire
6 April 2001

Head of Personnel
Kerrier District Council
Council Offices
Dolcoath Avenue
Cambourne TR14 8SX
Cornwall

Dear Sir/Madam

I am writing to you a most unusual letter, namely to apply for the position of 'Official Kerrier District Council Ghost Hunter and Exorcist' in the tradition of Parson Richard Dodge of the 1700s.

Aged 41, I have taken quite an interest in recent months in the many haunted sites and noted apparitions around the Cornwall region and believe I could offer an appropriate service in managing the ghosts and phantoms responsible for the aforementioned activity within your councils' jurisdiction.

As with all institutions the ethereal ghostly inhabitants of Cornwall would doubtless benefit from a more structured framework than exists at present and would permit a more co-ordinated and timed approach to entertaining-by-haunting the local people and indeed many visitors to the area. A predictable sighting [by efficient planning on my part] of Charlotte Dymond walking the slopes of Roughter, for example, would permit the rather satisfied observer more time to enjoy himself/herself at a local restaurant or theatre and by arranging the various Cornish Phantom Coaches to appear at specific times in various places a system could be introduced to allow the committed coach-watcher to enjoy several apparitions in a single night. As a consequence the various spirit entities would be fully occupied with less time to make nuisances of themselves, the human population given regular opportunities for trans-dimensional experiences, and moreover the tourism industry encouraged.

Should any particular disincarnate entity refuse to comply with such applied management strategy I am sure that the reputation of my experience in exorcism would be sufficient to deter further disorder or alternatively provide the means for eternal dismissal.

I have already had some psychic communication with 'Flo' of Duporth Holiday Village and, although bitter about the demolition of the old Manor, expressed her belief that my proposal for an ordered Cornish Otherworld community could well be a solution to the present chaos that exists in the county. Despite the opposition these changes will meet from some of the more discontent sprites and poltergeists I am of the opinion that the implementation of this new approach can be completed efficiently and with success should you employ me in the aforementioned capacity.

I would be most grateful for the chance to discuss this position with you further and thank you for your time and consideration.

Yours sincerely

Michael A. Lee

KERRIER DISTRICT COUNCIL

**Council Offices Dolcoath Avenue
Camborne Cornwall TR14 8SX**

Telephone:	Camborne (01209) 614000
Fax:	Camborne (01209) 614496
Email:	Geoff.Cox@kerrier.gov.uk
Web:	www.kerrier.gov.uk

Mr M A Lee
Somewhere in West Yorkshire

GEOFFREY G COX, LLB, Solicitor
Chief Executive Officer

Please ask for:	Mrs Chapman
Direct Dial:	01209 614362
Your Ref:	
My Ref:	MEC/pers
Date:	12 April 2001

Dear Mr Lee

Official Kerrier District Council Ghost Hunter and Exorcist

Thank you for your letter dated 6 April seeking employment by this Council in the above capacity.

As far as I am aware, the Council has never felt the need to make such an appointment so regret to say that I cannot help you at this time.

Thank you for your interest in the Kerrier District.

Yours sincerely

Margaret Chapman

Margaret Chapman
PA to the Chief Executive

Somewhere in West Yorkshire
29 April 2001

Dr M. J. Adam
Waterloo Surgery
615–619 Wakefield Road
Waterloo
Huddersfield

Dear Dr Adam

I am writing to you a most unusual letter, namely to apply for a position at Waterloo Health Centre as a Partner in General Practice.

Aged 41, I have been for many years a longstanding member of the Fell Runners Association. As such I am experienced in matters of map reading and believe this would be of great benefit when it comes to finding my way around the areas serviced by the Waterloo Practice.

Despite the complexity of the local road system around various parts of Huddersfield my accomplished navigational skills should overcome any challenges involved in home visits and indeed finding my way home after a long and stressful day at work.

In addition to a rather comprehensive file of fell race records demonstrating my tenacity at seeing a race through from its' beginning to its' end, a necessary characteristic for General Practice in these demanding times, I can also boast various swimming certificates assuring you of my ability to keep my head well above the water. Considering how much administration there is as an added necessity to the patient-orientated workload for the New Millennial family doctor this will doubtless serve as a useful survival trait should you employ me as your new partner.

Amongst my many other pastimes I have for some time now had a keen interest in gardening and have learned to tell the difference between the wood and the trees as well as recognise the shrubs and plants that possess hidden thorns. Along with a substantial knowledge that specific garden pests and diseases require specific treatments I believe that I can offer you assurance that I fully understand the need for a structure in General Practice that provides for efficient diagnosis and indeed medicinal or surgical solutions as appropriate.

Amongst my many books I have two sturdy volumes of the *Oxford Textbook of Medicine* which I believe will serve me well in aiding my diagnostic duties at Waterloo and although the majority of my writing has been in the field of job applications, I am sure I could write letters of referral when required.

... continued

As someone who has experienced various strains of the Common Cold, worried about mild anxiety connected to pressures at work and suffered from painful verrucae, I would be most able to empathise with 80 per cent of the patients visiting surgery on a daily basis. As far as the others are concerned I may require a little mentoring!

In summary I would be most interested to be considered as a General Practitioner in your highly regarded practice and despite my lack of any suitable medical qualification relevant to the aforementioned role I am sure my interests and experience would nevertheless serve me well in a somewhat liberal context.

I would like to take this opportunity of thanking you for your time and consideration and look forward to hearing from you in the very near future.

Sincerely and ambitiously

Michael A. Lee

Waterloo Surgery,
615-619, Wakefield Rd.,
Waterloo,
Huddersfield.
HD8 0LS

17th Sept 2001

Dear Mr. Lee,

I must apologise to you for not replying earlier to your frank and very interesting application for the position of partner at Waterloo Surgery as a partner in General Practice.

I regret to inform you that the post has now been filled but I feel that you would be interested to hear of my views on your wish to enter General Practice.

I do not see that your lack of a medical qualification should in any way bar you from pursuing this career. It has become very obvious that nowadays the patients know considerably more than the doctors they profess to consult and indeed, usually they get what they ask for. A GP's job now seems to be an aid to the technical and ludicrous notion that he or she alone can sign prescriptions, organise investigations and refer patients to hospital. The concept that the patient is 'God' and the patient 'knows best' is well established as evidenced by the 'lay down and kick me' attitude of the General Medical Council. I do not see you should have any difficulty convincing the authorities to enter General Practice – might I suggest that you buy a medical qualification in Dubai where I understand there is the biggest duty free outlet in the world- and respond to the Government's appeal for more doctors from abroad in the first place. This would certainly provide you with the appropriate certification to practice in this country and pursue your ambition.

I was most impressed by your achievements in fell running. In my opinion all fell runners are crackpots and let's face it you have to be mad to enter General Practice. I am not sure as to the usefulness of your swimming experience but certainly there is a vogue for underwater births and you may find this a specialty you might wish to develop or even expand e.g. underwater genito-urinary medicine or gynaecology. Clearly a life-saving certificate would circumvent the need for Cardiopulmonary Resuscitation accreditation – a bronze should suffice.

Administration is no problem. The state of the health service is such at the moment that it works entirely on the chaos theory principle. As such no one person or practice can be deemed to be accountable for anything, audits can be invented and the only requisite is the ability to be creative. Given the style of your application I do not think you will have much trouble here.

... continued

The interest in horticulture and garden pests and diseases will certainly be an asset to any practice fortunate to have you as a partner. General Practice does involve long periods of boredom so what better way of spending the time other than tending a garden. I am sure that a bid could be placed to the Primary Care Group for a therapeutic garden for the benefit of your patients on the assumption that they work in it for therapeutic reasons and so you should be saved the chores such as digging, weeding and grass cutting. In practice, plants and patients tend to suffer the same sort of problems e.g. wilt –'tired all the time' and mildew - Athletes foot, and will respond to similar treatments. A little inventiveness may be required but basically anything you use on plants will, as with patients, either kill or cure. I have often wondered what the human equivalent of 'Round-Up' would be. Perhaps there is an M.D. in this?

Don't worry about textbooks. They are far too thick, unreadable and unimaginably boring. Listen to the patients. They know it all and all you have to do is agree with them, get them to sign a disclaimer and hand them what they want. Patients always feel the best doctors are the ones that do what the patient wants.

NEVER admit to having an illness. In spite of your previous history of colds and verrucas, to admit to a patient that you are anything but superhuman and immune to all illness and therefore able to work 365 days a year non-stop 24 hours a day will beg the question whether you really are fit to practice and may land you in front of the General Medical Council. Similarly ditch this idea of empathy. It is like an infectious illness and you might find yourself developing symptoms and hypochondriacal ideas which may lead you to suspect that you are not really fit to practice –an absurd notion!

I hope that in spite of your disappointment in not being successful with your application to the Waterloo Practice that you will be reassured and I hope a little encouraged, or even inspired to become a General Practitioner and try again.

Best wishes for the future.

Yours sincerely,

Dr. M.J. Adam

Somewhere in West Yorkshire
4 May 2001

Head of Personnel
Penwith District Council
St Clare
Penzance TR18 3QW
Cornwall

Dear Sir/Madam

I am writing to you a most unusual letter, namely to apply for the position with Penwith District Council of 'Jack the Giant Killer [the Second]' should this position become available in the near future.

Aged 41, I am presently employed as a sales executive within industry but have had for quite some time now a particular dislike for giants and their evil ways. I have also had a desire to relocate to the South West and have quite a liking for Cornwall. In these times of increasing criminal activity it angers me to think of cattle-stealing giants following in the ancient warped tradition of Cormoran of St Michaels' Mount and creating even more work for an already stretched police force not to mention providing a less than ideal role model for the youth of today. I am sure that you would agree that there is a clear need for both community vigilance and indeed someone at hand to fulfil the role of 'Jack' should there be a local Giant problem that requires immediate attention.

As a long-standing member of the Fell-Runners Association I am a fit individual well trained in the art of race and pursuit and am able to run for long periods of time and at a significant pace when the occasion arises. This is a useful ability when pursuing or indeed evading or ambushing giants that possess a large stride or urgency. In addition to my flight of foot, I am a keen gardener and as such am adept at digging efficiently so that should there be a requirement to excavate large pits for the purpose of trapping your troublesome giants I would certainly be the person for the job. In terms of despatching the aforementioned giants, once again I am suitably qualified as a strong and determined individual and would not be averse to tapping these enormous criminal brutes on the head as did the original Jack. [I may need to acquire from one of your local council services a suitable pickaxe for this purpose.]

I am fully aware that unlike the time of the original Jack there are few if any wolves or pirates remaining in Cornwall, and so I realise that my responsibilities would be relatively restricted to the larger pests in the area. However, doubtless it would be fair to say that from a cost-effectiveness perspective my role would be fully justified as far as savings to police-time, livestock and indeed copycat behaviour is concerned if just one troublesome giant was culled in a particular season.

In conclusion, I am looking forward to the opportunity of discussing this matter with you further and thank you for your time and consideration.

Yours sincerely

Michael A. Lee

Penwith District Council

St. Clare Penzance Cornwall TR18 3QW
Telephone (01736) 362341 Fax (01736) 336575
Jim McKenna BA CPFA **Chief Executive**

David Hooper LL.B(Hons) Solicitor
Head of Legal and Personnel Services

Your Ref:
My Ref: DAG/CGE
Ask For: **MRS D A GROVES**
Direct Dial: (01736) 336536
Date: 25 April 2001

Dear Mr Lee

RE: POSITION OF "JACK THE GIANT KILLER (THE SECOND)"

Thank you for your recent offer of availability for employment if the above position should become created.

Fortunately, for us, our Giants although temperamental can be quite reasonable and we see no need for a slayer of Giants at this particular time.

If however, in the future, our resident Giants become unruly any such vacancy would be advertised through our local employment service and in the local press therefore reference to these from time to time is recommended.

In the meantime, good luck with your Giant killing!

Yours sincerely

PP · *[signature]*

Personnel Officer

Mr M A Lee
Somewhere in West Yorkshire

Somewhere in West Yorkshire
14 May 2001

Tony Blair
The Prime Minister
10 Downing Street
London SW1A 2AA

Dear Mr Blair

I am writing to you a most unusual letter, namely to apply for the position within the present government of 'Official Scapegoat'.

There have been numerous occasions over the last few years when I have switched on my television to hear the evening news or indeed read with interest various articles about current governmental policy within the national press to find the word 'scapegoat' bandied about. It seems to me as if there is always someone, often sat in either the Conservative or Liberal Democrats Party, keen to find a particular individual on whose shoulders the responsibility and blame for decisions made by the Labour Government but that find opposition elsewhere can be firmly placed. Much time and energy is devoted to this hunt for the so-called 'Scapegoat' as illustrated most graphically by coverage of the closure of Wembley Stadium recently but never have I heard of anyone actually claiming responsibility and accountability for such a role.

How handy it would be to have a particular person at whom the hordes of bitter dissenters could point and wag their bony fingers whenever the need arises!

On this basis I presume there is a vacancy for which I would like to be considered and provided that there would not be included in the terms and conditions of the job an expectation to bare any financial or legal penalties associated with duties undertaken, I would like to become the 'Official Scapegoat' forthwith.

Aged 41, I am currently employed within industry as a Sales Representative and as such am resilient and thick-skinned. In so saying I would be able to bare the brunt of many policy criticisms on behalf of the government far better than the average person. I am also a skilled communicator and would be a competent choice when it comes to explaining to those in the accusers chairs why exactly I am taking the blame for a particular unpopular decision or resolution. Although I do need a new pair of quality shoes for the role, I can assure you that I am of a smart, intelligent appearance and believe I would prove to be a highly efficient and popular scapegoat should I be successful in my application.

As a longstanding member of the Fell Runners Association I can assure you that I am able to 'go the distance ' and my possession of various swimming certificates should offer proof that I can easily keep my 'head above water'. Amongst the usual assortment of GCE 'O' Levels, 'A' Levels and degree, I also have a Garden Design Certificate which would serve me well in deciding how exactly to construct a watertight story or a retaining excuse that will effectively prevent a political landslide. In short and in figurative terms I could be the pond-liner in the great government lake of Westminster!

I thank you for your time and kind consideration regards my application for the position of 'Official Scapegoat' and look forward to hearing from you in the very near future.

Sincerely

Michael A. Lee

1O DOWNING STREET
LONDON SW1A 2AA

From the Direct Communications Unit   23 May 2001

Mr Michael A Lee
Somewhere in West Yorkshire

Dear Mr Lee

The Prime Minister has asked me to thank you for your recent
letter.

Yours sincerely

AEMER LODHI

Somewhere in West Yorkshire
15 May 2001

Her Royal Majesty The Queen
Buckingham Palace
London

Your Royal Highness

I am writing to you a most unusual letter, namely to apply for the position within the House of Lords of 'Principal Prodder and Nudge-Master'.

Having observed with great interest on many occasions the gatherings of our many eminent Lords, Ladies, Earls and other titled persons within the House of Lords I have been regularly amazed at the number of individuals who have clearly nodded off to sleep in the midst of the proceedings. Whilst, on one side of the House a learned Baron provides his fellow Lords with the latest information around the dangers of atmospheric pollutants on the worlds' ozone layer, three or four other members of the House are away in the 'Land of the Sandman' totally embroiled in a pleasant dream or snoring contentedly after an earlier glass of sherry or port.

Despite the vast number of people listed as Principal Officers and Officials within the House of Lords holding a miscellany of titles ranging from 'Lord Chancellor' through 'Counsel to the Chairman of the Committees' to 'Principal Doorkeeper' I can find no-one whose job it is to wake the Lords from their slumbers and ensure their leadership is not lost to the Land of Nod.

Aged 41, I have spent half a career in industry and consider myself an industrious, conscientious, astute and moreover alert individual and believe that it is of benefit to any team proceedings to have fully conscious members who can play a full part in the work at hand. Blessed with a loud voice and reasonably bony fingers I am sure I would be a most efficient candidate for a role which involved rousing a sleeper from his alternative state of mind by a short, sharp shout in the ear and a prod in the ribs.

As a rather tenacious individual, I am not one for giving up on a task easily and even those who have perhaps added a little too much whisky to their water would not be too much of a challenge to me.

As 'Principal Prodder and Nudge-Master' at the House of Lords I am sure I could ensure an attendance of Lords who would become brighter eyed, bushier tailed and more capable of at least appearing to help lead the House in the way they are expected to.

Doubtless you would agree with me that this role would carry significant responsibility and would certainly require a character of the highest calibre and commitment. I believe I am that person!

I thank you for your time and kind consideration and I look forward to hearing from you in the very near future.

Sincerely

M. A. Lee

Michael A. Lee

BUCKINGHAM PALACE

21st May, 2001

Dear Mr. Lee,

Thank you for your recent letter to The Queen suggesting that your particular skills would be appropriate for the mythical post of *Principal Prodder and Nudgemaster* in the House of Lords. Your thoughtfulness in putting your name forward for this office is appreciated, but it is not within the gift of the Palace and so it would seem you will have to dream on .....

Yours sincerely,

MRS. DEBORAH BEAN
Chief Correspondence Officer

M.A. Lee, Esq.

Lieutenant General Sir Michael Willcocks KCB

GENTLEMAN USHER OF THE BLACK ROD
HOUSE OF LORDS LONDON SW1A OPW

TEL: 020-7219 3100
FAX: 020-7219 2500

30 May 2001

Dear Mr Lee,

Thank you for your letter in which you apply for the position of Principal Prodder and Nudge-master. I am afraid that at present there is no such vacancy.

To be fair to the Members, however, I should point out that the acoustics in the Chamber are dreadful and to counteract this loudspeakers have been set into the backs of the benches. What may appear to the general public therefore as sleepy postures are actually the result of the Member in question having to position his/her ear to the nearest loudspeaker in order to catch the debate.

I wish you luck in your quest for service to the Nation.

Yours sincerely,

Michael Willcocks

GENTLEMAN USHER OF THE BLACK ROD

Michael A Lee Esq
Somewhere in West Yorkshire

Somewhere in West Yorkshire
24 May 2001

The Marketing Director
The Dulux Dept/ICI Paints
Abbott Mead Vickers – BBDO Ltd
151 Marylebone Road
London NW1 5QE

Dear Sir/Madam

I am writing to you a most unusual letter, namely to apply for the position of 'Hairy Human Dulux Dog' to feature in your well-respected paint adverts on TV and in various magazines as appropriate.

Along with many other people in the UK I have been a longstanding admirer of your highly successful advertising scheme involving the loveable Dulux dog and I suppose it is fair to say that the image of the dog has become synonymous with your brand of paints.

My only concern regards your canine Dulux dog adverts is that, whilst appealing to a large section of dog-loving UK residents, it may not actually convert to usage of Dulux paints the many individuals who are either neutral towards mans' best friend or indeed actually dislike the creature with a vengeance. Could it be that whilst gaining a certain allegiance of one section of the population to your paints you may actually be discouraging another pool of potential customers from using your products and perhaps even losing them to the competition? Having so defined a need in the paint advertising market place let me therefore propose a solution to you!

Aged 41, I am a rather weathered but friendly looking Northerner with a reasonable level of fitness and blessed with a rug-like preponderance of ginger-brown body hair across my back, chest, shoulders and arms. One might say that I am slightly reminiscent of a hairy domestic dog exuding a certain primal enthusiasm and energy whilst at the same time adding a very human element to the equation and image.

My proposal is simply this – employ me as your next advertising image: the 'Hairy Human Dulux Dog' and I could add an extra dimension of memorability and sales potential for your existing customers whilst encouraging those previously unconvinced by the original dog or dogs to think more kindly of a paint associated with a real person, be it a rather hairy wolven one. By adding to your original theme whilst injecting a measure of humour you might well find that demand for your Dulux paints quickly increases and the year-end sales bonuses become very attractive indeed!

I can hold a paintbrush between my teeth and would be quite willing to appear in a range of colours to suit the marketing strategies at any particular time. I would also be able to jump through the occasional hoop if necessary.

I can already visualise the upturn of the Dulux cash sales growth in my mind's eye!

Doubtless you will want to discuss this idea further with me at some point in the very near future and perhaps we could meet at an appropriate time and place for a bowl of something thirst-quenching and a juicy steak. I thank you for your time and consideration and look forward to hearing form you in the very near future.

Sincerely

M . A . Lee

Michael A. Lee
52

ABBOTT MEAD VICKERS · BBDO LTD

151 Marylebone Road
London NW1 5QE
Telephone 020 7616 3500
Fax 020 7616 3600
amvbbdo@amvbbdo.com

June 21, 2001

Michael Lee
Somewhere in West Yorkshire

Dear Mr Lee

Application for Dog Role

Thank you for your letter dated 24th May.

We were most interested to read of your market insights concerning non-dog loving paint users, and intrigued by your proposal to audition for a role as 'the Hairy Human Dulux Dog'.

Whilst we do not anticipate the immediate demise of our current canine talent, we are grateful for your concern over our future options.

Holding a paintbrush between your teeth would certainly be a minimum performance requirement. However, some 46% of paint is now applied via roller. Are there any innovative tricks you can perform with one of these?

Best wishes

Yours sincerely

Tom Nester-Smith
Board Account Director – ICI Paints

Registered in England
Registration Number
1935786
Registered Office
151 Marylebone Road
London NW1 5QE

Head of Personnel
Pendle Borough Council
Town Hall
Market Street
Nelson
Pendle BB9 7LG
Lancashire

Dear Sir/Madam

I am writing to you a most unusual letter, namely to apply for the position of 'Witchfinder General' for Pendle Borough Council.

I would be most interested indeed to follow in the footsteps of Mathew Hopkins of the 17th century whom I believe was born in the town of Manningtree within the boundaries of Tendring District Council, Essex, but who had an enormous effect on life around the Pendle area and whose role is currently vacant.

Aged 41, I have for quite some time been significantly concerned about the upsurge of interest in matters related to the occult by large numbers of people within the UK and particularly those involved in the ancient practice of Witchcraft. Only last week I was myself the witness of a troublesome incident here in the North of England when my sister-in-law visited the home of my wife and I one warm and humid afternoon. On her departure and to my great distress I found that the milk had curdled on top of the fridge, my prize daffodils had irreversibly drooped and all the family was struck down with an almost unearthly thirst. Having tentatively mentioned these occurrences and my understandably well-founded suspicions of my sister-in-law's leanings towards the dark arts to my dearly beloved, I then found that my wife could not bring herself to speak to me for almost a month. Isn't this appalling? Quite frankly I am shocked to think that such obvious sorcery and demonic spellbinding is so evident and even permissible in today's so-called civilised 21st-century England!

I understand from my research of times past that the approach towards finding women of the kind mentioned above was rather different to that of present times and similarly that the penalties for the practice of such devilry were far more severe if proven. Indeed it is interesting to read of the fate of the infamous witches of Pendle in Lancashire or those of Chelmsford four hundred years ago.
Should my sister-in-law, who incidentally also lives in Lancashire, have had the opportunity to consider that her fate could be a similar one to that of the Pendle or Chelmsford Witches if she did not return to the righteous path, I am convinced that the milk on the fridge would still be fresh and the daffodils in full flower.

In addressing my concerns I trust that you can now see my reasoning for applying to be the new 'Witchfinder General' and will be suitably convinced that the re-establishment of this role would be pivotal in dowsing the wiccan embers once and for all.

Having spent half a career in the world of industry I am experienced in the techniques

... continued

of interviewing people. This would indispensable in my role as 'Witchfinder General' both in terms of recruiting my team of 'Witchfinder Technicians' and also within the process of extracting confessions from those practicing their evil ways either on a solitary basis or as part of a larger coven. I am reasonably strong and believe that once my suspects are found and captured I could easily bind them prior to undertaking the well-known water test; if they sink they are innocent and if they float they can be justifiably hung, burned at the stake or perhaps more appropriately in 2001 be given the obligation of community service.

I know that the great Witchfinder General of the 1600s, Mathew Hopkins, received just twenty shillings for each witch he discovered and of course at that time this would have been an ample reward for his efforts. Should I be successfully appointed as his 21st-century successor I believe we would need to discuss further the salary and bonus package taking into consideration factors of inflation and job equivalents. There is also the matter of obtaining an appropriate uniform.

Doubtless you will be interested to take this application forward to the interview stage and with such in mind I would be grateful if you could send to me details about the selection process.

I thank you for your time and consideration and look forward to hearing from you in the very near future.

Sincerely

Michael A. Lee

CORPORATE POLICY UNIT
Town Hall, Market Street, Nelson, Pendle, Lancashire BB9 7LG

Telephone:	**(01282) 661984**	Fax:	**(01282) 661630**
Ext:		My Ref:	
Ask for:	Sarah Lee	Your Ref:	
Date:	18 June 2001		

Somewhere in West Yorkshire

Dear Mr Lee,

Thank you for your letter promoting yourself as a Witchfinder General, although I think you may be several centuries too late.

I'm enclosing a Pendle Discovery Guide so that you can find our more about the Pendle Witches of 1612.

At the back of the guide is a mail order section where you can order any publications about the witches, including a Pendle Witches Trail guide. We also have an audio guide to the Pendle Witches Trail which you can contact our Tourist Information Centre about (address and telephone number on inside back cover).

The world famous trial documents of the Pendle Witches were used as a guide by the Witchfinder General. However, I understand that he himself was executed as a witch some years later, which might make you re-think your position.

With best wishes,

Sarah Lee
Principal Promotions Officer

Corporate Policy Manager: Brian Astin
Switchboard: (01282) 661661   Minicom: (01282) 618392   Fax:(01282) 661630

Somewhere in West Yorkshire
29 June 2001

Head of Communications
Michelin Tyre PLC
Campbell Road
Stoke-on-Trent ST4 4EY

Dear Sir/Madam

I am writing to you a most unusual letter, namely to apply for the position of 'Michael the Merry Mobile Michelin Man' with Michelin Tyres PLC.

Aged 41, I have spent many years working as a sales executive within British industry and have reached that crossroads in life where I am exploring other potential career pathways. In this regard I was most interested to read on your website that 'ongoing individual career plans and personal progress are fundamental to the Michelin philosophy' and decided on this basis that you would be an excellent choice for my employment aspirations.

The Michelin Man logo and model has been a longstanding and memorable part of the Michelin Tyre business and I doubt that there would be many individuals unfamiliar with such a unique and outstanding image. I firmly believe, however, that you could further strengthen the business generated by such an image by employing an individual like myself to fulfil the role of 'Michael the Merry Mobile Michelin Man' in a human capacity at various exhibitions, PR events and occasions of hospitality. In other words, you could bring to life your logo in the same way that Disneyland has brought to life the cartoons Mickey Mouse and friends for thousands to see and with whom they can interact. The implications as far as sales promotion are concerned would doubtless be significant.

I would encourage you to consider me for this position on the basis of the following characteristics, skills and competencies.

First and foremost, my first name is Michael and so there would be no great challenge in my coming to terms with being addressed as 'Michael the Merry Mobile Michelin Man.' It might of course be a more complex process if I were a Cedric, Hubert or Zachariah!

Secondly, I have a natural propensity for weight-gain around the stomach and as in so saying would provide a basic costume-friendly shape for a Michelin Man outfit. Indeed individuals would notice, and quite rightly so, that 'Michael the Merry Mobile Michelin Man' not only promotes spare tyres, but even carries them around himself! I am sure that you would agree this would be an ideal association to encourage.

Thirdly, I can assure you that as a longstanding member of the Fell Runners Association I am a relatively fit, be it slightly overweight, man with a substantial mobility and stamina. This would serve me well in the capacity of attending events of reasonable duration where there would be an expectation for committed socialising and promotional effort to take place. One might say 'I can go round for a long time!'

… continued

Finally, I have had a longstanding interest in tyres in their many forms and as a consequence could bring to the role a natural enthusiasm and interest that would help in the promotion of the company, Michelin Tyres PLC, and its well-established product range. I perform well under reasonable pressure and have no history of personal punctures.

I thank you for your time and consideration in relation to my job application and I look forward to hearing from you in the very near future.

Sincerely

M. A. Lee

Michael A. Lee

Mr M A Lee
Somewhere in West Yorkshire

24 July 2001

Dear Mr Lee

Job application - Michelin Man

Thank you for your two letters dated 29 June recently received in this office. Your notion of 'Michael the Merry Mobile Michelin Man' is novel, to say the least! Over the years we have used Michelin men (and women) to wear our Bibendum (Michelin Man) suits for the types of function which you highlight in your letter. Today, these suits are made in the USA and considerably easier to wear than the stiff nylon ones of the 1960s-90s. It has therefore become easier to press-gang our volunteer employees, often apprentices, in to action!

We note your offer and should our Michelin men and women 'go on strike', we'll make contact!

Yours sincerely

Paul Niblett
Head of Communications

paul.niblett@uk.michelin.com

Michelin Tyre
Public Limited Company

Tel: +44 (0)1782 402000
Fax: +44 (0)1782 402011

Campbell Road
Stoke-on-Trent
ST4 4EY

Website: www.michelin.co.uk
Registered in England no. 84559
Registered Office: Stoke-on-Trent ST4 4EY

INVESTOR IN PEOPLE

The Chairman
The Ancient Order of Foresters
Friendly Society
904–910 High Road
North Finchley
London N12 9RW

Dear Sir/Madam

I am writing to you a most unusual letter, namely to enquire about the possibility of being employed by the Ancient Order of Foresters Friendly Society as a 'Woodsman'.

Aged 41, I have spent many years as a sales executive within the British Industry but have reached that time of life when I am exploring alternative employment opportunities. Indeed I have recently begun considering a return to the work I was involved in on the North Yorkshire Estate of Aldwark, now National Trust I believe, where I spent many months trimming branches from coniferous trees and clearing drainage ditches with a billhook and a scythe shortly after graduating in 1981. Although the weather was harsh, the salary poor and conditions challenging there was a certain contentment associated with a hard days work in the woods and certain benefits as far as physical fitness and harmony with nature were concerned. Indeed I look back with a certain pleasurable nostalgia at my time as an Estate Woodsman.

As you will doubtless understand I was therefore significantly excited at discovering your organisation on the Internet and although I have not fully absorbed all the information on your well-presented website, I decided you may well be an ideal choice for my application for a return to the trees.

I am an affable, industrious, conscientious and well-educated individual with 18 years of scientific sales beneath my career belt but more importantly am fit and strong and already experienced in many techniques of forestry maintenance and management. Although my recent career has been one of involvement with health-care professionals I am just as able to communicate easily and clearly with farmers, fire-fighters and local village families. In short, I would be an ideal candidate to consider for the position of 'Woodsman' with your organisation.

I noticed also that there was an entry on your website describing 'The Band' of The Ancient Order of Foresters Friendly Society and may I take this opportunity to say that should you be short of musicians I am also something of a dab hand at playing the kazoo. Indeed I often play my kazoo here in our leafy garden in Huddersfield.

Thank you for your time and consideration as far as this application is concerned and I look forward to hearing from you in the very near future.

Sincerely

M. A. Lee

Michael A. Lee

Ancient Order of Foresters Friendly Society

London United District
Foresters House, 904-910 High Road, Finchley, London N12 9RW
Telephone: 020-8445 8878 Fax: 020-8343 8510
E-mail:lud@aof.co.uk

Friends you can trust

Our Ref:	Your Ref:
GDL/BP	

Mr M A Lee
Somewhere in West Yorkshire

19th July 2001

Dear Mr Lee,

Thank you for your letter dated 12th July 2001 and the information contained therein.

Unfortunately, I am unable to assist you with employment as the Society does not need "Woodsmen" nor does it require it a kazoo player in its Brass Band.

However, may I take this opportunity to enclose a leaflet, which gives a brief history of the Society and I wish you every success with your quest for an alternative career.

Yours sincerely,

G D Lloyd
District Secretary

Somewhere in West Yorkshire
24 July 2001

H. E. Mr Tarald O. Brautaset
Ambassador to the Court of St James
Royal Norwegian Embassy
25 Belgrave Square
London SW1X 8QD

Dear Sir

I am writing to you a most unusual letter, namely to ask whether I might purchase or lease the Island of Jan Mayen from the Norwegians who currently own and govern this most interesting land in a bid to fulfil my desire to become a 'Recluse'.

Aged 41, I have for some time been looking for an unusual piece of real estate that I might acquire on either a freehold or leasehold basis which would offer me a significant degree of peace and solitude. As the father of two small children and having a demanding wife, I have often dreamed of the type of island typified by Jan Mayen as a place for refuge and respite. In other words I am looking for a holiday home with a difference!

As a place located between the Greenland and Norwegian Seas at 71 00 North and 8 00 West and enjoying an arctic maritime climate with frequent storms and persistent fog, I believe there is little risk of mass tourism spoiling the remote nature of Jan Mayen. Indeed I gather that, with the exception of a few brave souls manning the meteorological station located on the island, there is absolutely no indigenous population whatsoever to interfere with the natural environment and its' intrinsic character.

Since Jan Mayen offers no natural resources, has no arable land, no crops, no pastures and no woodland but instead presents simply as a barren volcanic island of moss and grass, I can see no possible reason why the Norwegian Crown and government would want to maintain ownership of the island when presented with an offer of purchase or lease such as mine.

Should you be happy to proceed with the sale or lease of Jan Mayen as I fully expect you to do may I assure you that I will be quite happy for you to continue with your meteorological endeavours and indeed maintain the one airport that offers access to the interior. I would also be more than happy to permit any scientists interested in studying the active volcano Haakan V11 Tapen/Beerenberg to visit whenever they wished.

As for myself I would be most content to have free range to pitch my tent wherever I wanted on this most fascinating of islands and perhaps build a modest cabin for the more inclement times of the year where I could rest and meditate with at least a degree or two of comfort. I can think of no better place than Jan Mayen in which I could avoid my many household chores here in the North of England and permit my eardrums, damaged by many decibels of small children shouting over long periods of time, to recuperate and recover.

May I suggest that should you be happy to proceed with my purchase option a sum of £10 be paid for freehold possession forthwith and should you be more comfortable with the idea of a leasing contract that we run with 50p per year.

Many thanks indeed for your time and consideration regarding this matter and I look forward to hearing from you in the very near future.

In the meantime I had better go and entertain my family or I will be in serious trouble again.

Sincerely

M. A. Lee

Michael A. Lee

ROYAL NORWEGIAN EMBASSY
LONDON

Enquiries to

Our Date	Our Reference
27 July 2001	
Your Date	Your Reference
24 July 2001	

Mr Michael A Lee
Somewhere in West Yorkshire

Dear Mr Lee,

I am writing in reply to the generous offer contained in your letter of 24 July to the Norwegian Ambassador.

While appreciating your predicament, the Embassy regrets to inform you that the island of Jan Mayen is currently not up for sale nor lease. However, should there be any changes in this situation, you will probably be among the first to be notified.

In the meantime, you might like to consider spending a holiday on the Norwegian mainland, and I enclose "The official travel guide Norway 2001" for your perusal.

Yours sincerely,

Erik Svedahl
1st Secretary

Postal Address:
25 Belgrave Square
London
SW1X 8QD
Great Britain

Office Address:
25 Belgrave Square
London
SW1X 8QD
Great Britain

Telephone:
(+44) (0)20 7591 5500

Telefax:
(+44) (0)20 7245 6993

Website:
http://www.norway.org.uk

E-mail:
emb.london@mfa.no

63

Somewhere in West Yorkshire
1 August 2001

The Archbishop of Canterbury
Lambeth Palace
London SE1 7JU

Dear Sir

I am writing to you a most unusual letter, namely to apply for the position of 'Principal Stable Boy for the Four Horses of the Apocalypse'.

Having recently re-read parts of the Book of Revelation I was fascinated to consider the four horses that are described in Chapter Six and their pivotal but certainly unenviable roles in carrying around the four horsemen who are to be given power over a quarter of the earth in the last days. I am particularly perturbed at the thought of these white, black, red and pale horses having to play host to four individual horsemen who, we are told in verse eight, will kill people by war, starvation, disease and wild animals. What a mean team of heartless souls they must be! Quite frankly I would not wish to meet any of them on a dark night!

With respect to the horses, however, I assume that whilst they await their future briefings at the opening of the first of seven seals they will require kind and committed attention. In this regard employ me as 'Principal Stable Boy for the Four Horses of the Apocalypse' and I will ensure that these animals are suitably groomed, their saddles and bridles cleaned and polished, their shoes maintained and that they are properly fed and watered on a regular basis.
You can also rest assured that the horses will be suitable exercised and prepared for their release at the end of time in accordance with the graphic descriptions in the aforementioned chapter of Revelation.

Although, as Principle Stable Boy, mine would be primarily a role of equine care perhaps I might also assume a secondary and rather crafty role in supporting a more positive and caring approach to humanity. One could almost describe the role as that of an undercover agent in the apocalyptic stable. In short I could attempt to convince the horsemen themselves whilst visiting their respective steeds to desist from their obsessive interest in war, disease, starvation and nasty animals and concentrate on more wholesome interests such as jogging, fishing, poetry-writing and watercolour painting instead!

If I am successful the prophesied terrors of Revelation Chapter Six may be transformed into a future realism of worldwide self development, new interest and communities of people busy studying at evening classes and involving themselves in more endearing activities. The horses could be re-deployed to riding schools or put out to pasture and the horsemen become role models of true repentance.

Aged 41, I am an individual of tremendous vision and indeed focus. You will find me an industrious and conscientious person possessing a polished eloquence and positive attitude. Moreover I have a particular interest in apocalyptic issues and a desire to ameliorate the consequence of worldwide cataclysm if at all possible. Finally, I am fit and strong so that I might undertake my responsibilities with energy and efficiency, and should one of the horsemen take a particular dislike to me I can put up a jolly good fight.

Many thanks indeed for your time and kind consideration and I look forward to hearing from you in the very near future.

Sincerely

Michael A. Lee

Mr Michael A Lee
Somewhere in West Yorkshire

Mr Andrew Nunn
Lay Assistant to
The Archbishop of Canterbury

3 August 2001

Dear Mr Lee

The Archbishop of Canterbury has now left London for his summer break and so I am writing on his behalf to thank you for your 1 August letter. Thank you for putting your name forward for the position of Principal Stable Boy for the Four Horses of the Apocalypse. I regret however that applications for this post are not being handled from this office; the Archbishop is not regarded as the managing employer in this case. Rather you should apply to St John the Divine, c/o The Lamb and Flag, Patmos, Greece. If you are successful in your application, I am sure there will be many who will be grateful for any ameliorating influence you can bring to bear on the Horsemen, in the manner you propose.

Another position you may like to consider – but again the post is not in the Archbishop's gift – is that of stable boy to Balaam's Ass. Though less well remunerated than the position of Principal Stable Boy for the Four Horses of the Apocalypse and perhaps lacking the apocalyptic element that may be of crucial interest to you, this post represents a major opportunity in the field of animal welfare. In this case a history of cruelty and abuse means that the successful candidate must be able to demonstrate a proven track record in palliative equine care. Applications may be sent to Balaam son of Beor, Pethor near the River, Amaw.

With best wishes

Lambeth Palace, London SE1 7JU
Direct Line: +44(0)20 7898 1276 *Switchboard:* +44(0)20 7898 1200 *Fax:* +44(0)20 7261 9836
Email: andrew.nunn@lampal.c-of-e.org.uk

65

Somewhere in West Yorkshire
5 August 2001

Jim Cunningham
MP for Coventry South
The House of Commons
London SW1A 0AA

Dear Sir

I am writing to you a most unusual letter, namely to apply for the position of 'The Horse for Lady Godiva' should there be a requirement for such a role in the near future. As MP for Coventry South I thought that you might be the best person to approach for advice with regard to this position.

I am sure that the various carnivals and commemorative events that take place from time to time in the Coventry area providing the public with a theatrical glimpse of that most infamous Midlands maiden will have no end of well-qualified candidates for the part of Lady Godiva herself. I wondered, however, whether this would be the case when it comes to considering likely human candidates for the part of the horse if indeed a real horse is no longer an option.

Considering the current foot and mouth disaster that has restricted the movement of so many animals in so many places I would suggest that it would be far more appropriate to select an appropriate person to fill this role for forthcoming occasions as we move forward into late summer and autumn.

In this regard, I can assure you that I would be an ideal candidate for any events requiring a horse for Lady Godiva and would certainly like to be considered for such.

Aged 41, I am a moderately large but fit individual with a thick covering of ginger-brown body hair. As a member of the Fell Runners Association I am accomplished at completing various paced runs and courses and would be adept at 'trotting', 'cantering' and indeed 'galloping' when appropriate. Furthermore, I would be quite willing for the female playing the part of Lady Godiva to sit on my muscular back whilst I parade with joyful whinnying through the streets of Coventry.

I am a fit and healthy individual and apart from my 'Athletes Foot' which is well contained I have no other communicable diseases that would be of concern to the local population.

I would be most pleased to provide you with a copy of my CV if you wish to take this application process forward.

May I say, however, that should my services be required I would need a firm offer of employment as soon as possible as various other organisations have expressed significant interest in my obvious career aspirations and flexibility and in this regard there is substantial interest in my becoming the new Beast of Bodmin Moor or possibly the new mascot for the Parachute Regiment.

Between ourselves I must say that I would prefer working more closely with a charming Lady Godiva in Coventry than either the angry, war-hungry men of Aldershot or wandering the bleak and lonely heights of Bodmin Moor with no fixed abode. In these difficult times, however, one needs to keep options open.

I thank you for your time and consideration and look forward to hearing from you in the very near future.

Sincerely and hopefully

Michael A. Lee

66

JIM CUNNINGHAM MP
COVENTRY SOUTH

HOUSE OF COMMONS
LONDON SW1A 0AA

Immigration Assistant:
Liz Hasthorpe
Tel: (024) 7625 7870
Fax: (024) 7625 7813

Constituency Office:
Tel/Fax: (024) 7655 3159
London Office:
Tel/Fax: (020) 7219 6362

JC/PB

15th August, 2001.

Mr. M.A. Lee,
Somewhere in West Yorkshire

Dear Mr. Lee,

Thank you for your recent letter offering your services as "The Horse for Lady Godiva" at any carnivals or commemorative events that may take place in Coventry.

I have forwarded a copy of your letter onto the City Centre Company (Coventry) Limited, New Union Street, Coventry, who promote such events in the City.

My secretary has spoken to the Company, who have advised her that the Carnival has not been held in Coventry for some time, but that that your letter would be kept on record, should any events occur in the future.

Yours sincerely,

Jim Cunningham, MP
COVENTRY SOUTH

CITY CENTRE COMPANY
COVENTRY

M.A.Lee Esq.

Somewhere in West Yorkshire

Lady Godiva's Horse

Dear Mr. Lee,

A copy of your letter to Jim Cunningham, MP re the above has been forwarded to me for my attention.

Your offer has some interesting possibilities and given your CV stands scrutiny with the Royal Veterinary Society I would be delighted to pursue the matter further.

I should however bring one important point to your notice. It is not well known by people outside the Coventry area but Lady Godiva's horse was never a "whole" animal. A prerequisite of any work we do with the delightful lady will be the necessity for you to be gelded, presupposing that has not already taken place of course.

I do hope the last item has not dampened your enthusiasm and look forward to receiving your CV in due course.

Liz Millett
Chief Executive

Cc H. Root

City Centre Company (Coventry) Limited · New Union Street
Coventry · CV1 2NT
Tel: 024 7683 3671/2   Fax: 024 7683 2017
www.coventry.towntalk.co.uk
Registered No: 3365320 Registered Office: The Council House · Earl Street · Coventry · CV1 5RR

Somewhere in West Yorkshire
19 August 2001

Liz Millett
Chief Executive
City Centre Company [Coventry] Ltd
New Union Street
Coventry CV1 2NT

Dear Ms Millett

First and foremost may I thank you for your recent letter dated 16 August in response
to my application for the role of 'The Horse for Lady Godiva'.

I am absolutely delighted to hear that my offer has 'interesting possibilities' and that should my
CV stand scrutiny with the Royal Veterinary Society, which I am confident it will as I am a most
credible creature, you will be delighted to pursue the matter further. I am not as delighted,
however, to hear that a prerequisite of my work within the role of 'The Horse for Lady Godiva'
would be for me to be gelded. In fact, such a notion brings tears to my eyes! Aged 41, I
consider myself to be at a prime time of my life and indeed am pleased to say that I am in
good condition and operational in every capacity and wish to remain so for many more years .

After considerable consideration I have come to the conclusion that the original horse for Lady
Godiva which, as you explained, was not a 'whole' animal must have been gelded on account
of a character which included an element of uncontrollable bestial behaviour. The poor fellow
was probably a little too frisky for his own good and I can fully understand why Lady Godiva
and her entourage would have been eager to err on the side of caution and remove any
possibility of the unthinkable.

In contrast, you may be relieved to learn that my own carnal nature has been trained and
disciplined over the years to conform only with convention and even though un-gelded I
would pose no immediate threat to the lovely Lady Godiva herself. At least not during public
events! If this information itself is not sufficient to convince you that I could still be employed
in the above capacity in my natural state, may I also suggest that for added peace of
mind you might provide me with a specially designed bridle which will prevent the raising
of unexpected interest in the lady in a mechanical manner.

In summary, although I do understand your initial suggestion regards emasculation, you
will hopefully be now reassured that you can employ me despite the necessary surgery
and rely instead on the well-honed discipline of a seasoned fell-runner and indeed on the
restraints of the bridling.

Doubtless you will now be keen to take this interview process to the next stage and I
look forward to hearing from you in the very near future.

Sincerely

Michael A. Lee
cc H.Root & his horse

Our Reference :
Direct Dialling No. :
Fax No. : 024 7683 1350
Date :
Reply to : 24 August 2001

CITY CENTRE COMPANY
COVENTRY

Mr M A Lee

Somewhere in West Yorkshire

Dear Mr Lee

LADY GODIVA'S HORSE

Thank you for your most recent letter regarding the above.

Unfortunately I had suspected that, as with other steeds before you, you would find difficulty in complying with the essential criteria of the job specification.

Whilst you offer a comprehensive account of your conformity to convention, it would be remiss of me to place Lady Godiva or the citizens of Coventry in a situation which may prove in any way unseemly, distressing, dangerous or illegal. You will recall that simply seeing the fair lady in a state of undress caused a permanent visual impairment to one of our previous residents. The risk is simply too great to contemplate.

However, whilst I have some difficulty in understanding your aversion to the knife, I am told that there are several products on the market which chemically can produce the same effect as physical gelding. May I invite you to consider this alternative route?

Yours sincerely

LIZ MILLETT
Chief Executive

City Centre Company (Coventry) Limited · New Union Street
Coventry · CV1 2NT
Tel: 024 7683 3671/2   Fax: 024 7683 2017
www.coventry.towntalk.co.uk
Registered No: 3365320 Registered Office: The Council House · Earl Street · Coventry · CV1 5RR

Coventry City Council

Members' Support Unit

Council House
Earl Street
Coventry
CV1 5RR

Please contact Janet Ford
Direct line 024 7683 1173
Fax 024 7683 1009
janet.ford@coventry.gov.uk

Mr M Lee
Somewhere in West Yorkshire

Our reference AL/jf/lee 2
16 October 2001

Dear Mr Lee

I have been asked by Mr Geoffrey Robinson MP to respond to your letter which was sent to him on 10 August 2001. I am the Cabinet Member (Area Co-ordination and Leisure) within Coventry City Council and therefore Mr Robinson feels that a response to your letter falls within my portfolio.

I must firstly apologise for the delay in responding to you but I have been away on holiday.

The post which you mention ie. 'The Horse for Lady Godiva', has been vacant for quite a number of years! After some research we believe that the salary which was last recorded for this post to be in the region of 3 bushels of hay, free stable and free horse shoes (up to a maximum of 4 sets per year).

I would be interested to receive your CV and specifically what attributes you can bring to this role and any references you are able to provide. Once I have received your CV, and should I consider you to be a suitable candidate, I shall contact you and invite you to Coventry for an audition. Perhaps we could ask Lady Godiva along to audition you.

I note that you mention that you suffer from athlete's foot and although you assure me that it is contained, I think it would be irresponsible if I did not request a 'Movement of Livestock' certificate from the Ministry of Rural Affairs if you were to visit Coventry.

I must say that sometimes my duties as Cabinet Member seem onerous but I look forward to receiving your CV and personally checking your fetlocks. I am a woman of indeterminate years and my fetlocks have been known to attract admiring glances but not for a number of years now!

Perhaps you could enclose a picture of yourself which may help us to decide if you are a suitable candidate?

I hope that you have not already been recruited by some other organisation and will be able to send me further information in the next few weeks.

Kind regards.

Yours sincerely

Councillor Mrs Ann Lucas
Cabinet Member (Area Co-ordination & Leisure)

Somewhere in West Yorkshire
7 August 2001

Sir Richard Body
MP for Boston & Skegness
The House of Lords
London

Dear Sir Richard

I am writing to you a most unusual letter, namely to ask how I might be considered for the position of 'Lincolnshire Poacher' should there be a suitable vacancy available at present or in the near future. As MP for Boston & Skegness I thought you would be the ideal person to whom I should turn for advice.

Inspired both by the fact that my father was from Lincolnshire and indeed by the images conveyed by the traditional folk song that shares the name of the job I am applying for, I believe that I would be an ideal candidate for the position.

Adept at walking and creeping around at night with little sound, I believe I could remain hidden and undetected for long periods of time in the copses and woods, hedgerows and ditches of the Lincolnshire countryside from both animals and indeed the gamekeepers. I have a love of the great outdoors and it could indeed be my delight on a moonlit night at any season of the year to stalk a prospective meal across the vast tracts of Lincolnshire farmland, riverbank and forest.

In terms of equipment there would be no need for you to worry about any cost to the local council; I have a full set of cold weather clothing, including a warm woolly hat, as well as appropriate gear for the warmer nights. I am a bit short when it comes to the department of tools used in the despatch of my quarry but will be only too pleased to acquire my own snares, ropes, knives and catapult. [A gun, I fear, would be too noisy!]

If you could advise me with reference to a place where I could buy a large thermos flask for the winter months ahead, I would be much obliged.

I thank you for your time and consideration and look forward to hearing from you in the very near future.

Sincerely

Michael A. Lee

Jewell's Farm,
Stanford Dingley,
Reading,
Berkshire,
RG7 6LX

August 15th
2001

Dear Mr Lee,

Thank you for your letter about being the Lincolnshire Poacher.

Ferreting is a good form of poaching. What experience of it have you?

If a gamekeeper catches you by surprise, you need to catch your ferret quickly and run with it.

How fast can you run with a ferret in your pocket?

Yours sincerely
Rinus Budy

Sir Richard Body
Jewells Farm
Stanford Dingley
Reading
Berkshire RG7 6LX

Dear Sir Richard

First and foremost, may I say thank you for your swift reply to my enquiries with regards to becoming 'The Lincolnshire Poacher'.

I wholeheartedly agree with your comments that ferreting is a 'good form of poaching' and has indeed proven itself an integral and popular element with many individuals within the poaching profession. My own experience of ferreting is, however, rather limited as I have a rare ferret phobia and consequently the associated fear of being savaged by these small but strong creatures has left me no option but to explore ferret-less techniques.

With respect to your valid and poignant question 'How fast can you run with a ferret in your pocket?' I hasten to add that I am a long-standing member of the Fell Runners Association and, although my track-record of running with a small furry creature in my pocket is a non-starter, I have been known to run for several hours on tough terrain and in inclement conditions at a reasonably noteworthy pace and often with a weighty rucksac on my back. When pursued by a worthy competitor during the odd fell race I can also report that my veins run thick with adrenalin and make my pursuit a most challenging endeavour for even the hardiest individual. The same would certainly be true in the event of my being caught by surprise by a vigilant gamekeeper.

In the light of this new information would you agree that my credentials for becoming the officially recognised 'Lincolnshire Poacher' are worthy enough for further consideration?

I trust that you will be interested to take my application for employment in the above capacity to the next stage and look forward to hearing from you in the very near future.

I will not be available for interview next week as I am having a short holiday to restore my catapult and clean my boots but will back in the throw of things the week beginning 3 September.

Sincerely

M. A. Lee

Michael A. Lee

Jewell's Farm,
Stanford Dingley,
Reading,
Berkshire,
RG7 6LX

August 24th
2001

Dear Mr Lee,

You seem hopelessly unqualified.

Yorkshiremen are world class timewasters.

Why not become The champion Yorkshire timewaster?

Write to every Yorkshireman your challenge to the title.

Once acclaimed the champion, a song will be written about you to be sung by millions.

Yours sincerely

Richard Ing

Somewhere in West Yorkshire
9 August 2001

Managing Director
Courts [UK] Ltd
The Grange
1 Central Road
Morden
Surrey SM4 5PQ

Dear Sir/Madam

I am writing to you a most unusual letter, namely to apply for the position of 'Courts' Jester' at a store of your choosing within the UK.

Having recently wandered around your Huddersfield store looking at various pieces of furniture and electrical goods it occurred to me that, despite present business appearing to be healthy, there may well be an unusual but memorable way for you to create further interest in your stores and merchandise and indeed increase overall business returns to an even greater extent.

Long ago in the courts of kings around various parts of the world, there were to be found colourfully dressed clowns or jesters whose job was to entertain the gatherings of people at state functions and generally add a little merriment to the proceedings at hand. Dressed in multicoloured costumes and often with accompanying bell-festooned hats of character and distinction these jesters would hop, dance and tumble their way around the courts making people laugh and adding to the spirit of the occasion.

Aged 41, I am an accomplished hopper, dancer and indeed tumble-turner and I can also sing like a lark, recite poetry and generate infectious laughter at will. As a long-standing member of the Fell Runners Association I have a significant strength and stamina and am able to maintain an energetic and vigorous mobility for long periods of time. In short, and in the absence of any Royal vacancies at present, I would make an ideal 'Courts Jester' whom the crowds of customers within your chosen store could watch and marvel and whose reputation and novelty would help attract an additional number of prospective purchasers to the store also.

Doubtless this concept will be of interest to you and perhaps you might consider piloting the position here in Huddersfield?

Should my jolly acrobatic antics be a success you might then wish to promote me to the position of 'Jester Recruitment and Training Executive' and permit me to interview and employ sufficient individuals of suitable character to jump, twist and twirl their individual ways throughout every Courts Store in the UK. Not only would your crowds of customers achieve their intended purchases and enjoy a certain shoppers' satisfaction but a trip to Courts could also become a multi-dimensional event and offer an additional element of circus for the benefit of the whole family. One can almost hear a small child saying to his father; 'Dad, please can we forget the theme park next week and come here again instead?' The father, in his wisdom, would reply of course, 'I'm glad you said that, son!'

… continued

Your sales would doubtless become a logarithmic growth phenomenon and those earning bonus and qualifying for shares will be chuffed to grollies. This is probably one of the few win-win suggestions you will hear in today's competitive market places.

I thank you for your time and consideration with regard to this unusual suggestion and I look forward to hearing from you in the very near future.

In the meantime I intend to add a few more bells and bobbles to my patchwork hat and will continue practicing my backward flips and ancient ballads with hope and commitment.

Sincerely

M. A. Lee

Michael A. Lee

PS I also juggle!

The Grange, 1 Central Road, MORDEN, Surrey, SM4 5PQ, United Kingdom
Telephone: 0208 640 3322 Fax 0208 410 9244
Direct Line: 0208 410 9381 Email: alison@COURTS.PLC.UK

21st August 2001

Mr M Lee
Somewhere in West Yorkshire

Dear Mr Lee

Thank you for your letter dated 9th August 2001, which has been passed to me for a response.

Reading through your letter I must firstly say how very impressed I was by the diversity and number of your skills. You are clearly a very talented man.

Although you do not mention salary in your letter we unfortunately have a policy of no new recruitment in the UK at the moment due to difficult trading conditions. It would also not be right to favour one store over another in the current climate so we would not be able to open a new position just in one store.

However, when we open new stores we are always looking for novel acts to keep children amused so maybe this is somewhere we would be able to work together? Perhaps you could send me a video of your 'act' and then I would be able to decide whether or not it would be suitable for our purposes.

Thank you again for taking the time to write to us.

Yours sincerely

Alison Cohen
PR Manager

Courts plc. Reg. No. 272534
Courts (UK) Ltd. Reg. No. 737130. Courts (Overseas) Ltd. Reg. No. 461239
All companies registered in England with registered offices at The Grange, 1 Central Road, Morden, Surrey SM4 5PQ

The Very Reverend C. Lewis
The Dean
The Deanery
Sumptor Yard
St Albans
Hertfordshire AL1 1BY

Dear Sir

I am writing to you a most unusual letter, namely to apply for the position of 'Gargoyle Model' for the Cathedral & Abbey Church of St Alban.

It was with great interest that I heard recently of the replacement of some of the traditional monstrous stone gargoyles around the outside of the Cathedral & Abbey Church of St Alban with new and appealing gargoyles depicting the faces of certain prominent 20th Century church figures and well-known individuals. I was immediately struck by the similarities of such an unusual development with the ways in which the Rotary Club or Round Table organisations choose their members from a variety of different backgrounds and professions.

In so saying, perhaps you would consider adding to your gargoyle collection of monsters and clergymen one or two stone depictions of a Yorkshireman with a business background famed for surviving a lightning strike six years ago and known locally for his fell-running and love of the hills.

Aged 41, I am an individual with a craggy face, misshapen nose, balding head and a less than handsome appearance. When on occasions I open my eyes in a wide, startling manner, my wife becomes rather nervous and usually scuttles off into another room to avoid my troublesome appearance. It is most disconcerting to be the one person in a city street of hundreds that small dogs always attack and at whose appearance babies begin to scream!

In short, I would be an excellent choice of model on which a modern-day gargoyle could be based offering an element of contrasting professional background to the existing entourage whilst maintaining the tradition of grotesque looks and propensity for scaring away those elemental beings who have no business creating mischief near the Cathedral.

Doubtless you will be interested to consider this proposal further and I look forward to hearing from you in the very near future.

Many thanks for your time.

Sincerely

M. A. Lee

Michael A. Lee

CATHEDRAL AND ABBEY CHURCH OF SAINT ALBAN

Sumpter Yard, St Albans, Hertfordshire, AL1 1BY, UK

Direct Dial: 01727 890202   Evenings/weekends 01727 890203   Cathedral: 01727 860780   Fax: 01727 890227
email: dean@stalbanscathedral.org.uk

Mr Michael Lee

Somewhere in West Yorkshire

11 September 2001

Dear Mr Lee,

Thank you for your letter of 7th September and I think that is a wonderful idea. We will hold you as a gargoyle reserve, as we unfortunately are not currently in production.

There was once a party for people who had their picture on the front of Time magazine and one of the speakers, apparently, remarked on the fact that looking round it must be the only magazine which did not choose their cover people for their good looks.

Yours sincerely

Christopher Lewis

The Very Reverend Christopher Lewis *Dean*
The Deanery, Sumpter Yard, St Albans, AL1 1BY

Head of Marketing – Strongbow
Bulmers Worldwide
Plough Lane
Hereford HR4 0LE

Dear Sir/Madam

I am writing to you a most unusual letter, namely to apply for the position of 'Archer' within the marketing team working with Bulmers Strongbow Cider.

Aged 41, I have reached that stage of life where I am beginning to consider a change of career direction and pursue an alternative pathway which will offer new challenge and interest and perhaps include pursuits I would normally explore outside of my work .

In this regard I am pleased to inform you that not only am I a keen cider drinker but also somewhat accomplished in the ancient skill of archery. At the age of ten I purchased my very first bow and arrow set and, though inhibited in utilising the full potential of such ancient tools by black, plastic suckers on the end of the arrows, I very quickly became adept in the art of launching my arrows in a manner supportive of fast and straight flight. There were many other children of a similar age whose mothers demanded retribution from my own poor parents for the hair-loss that their offspring suffered when removing stuck-fast suckered arrows from their tender heads. Since I was eventually forced to leave home in a hurried and permanent fashion and take refuge in Storthes Hall Woods near Huddersfield, avoiding the many searches by the newly named One-Eyed Inspector Tallbody and his boys in blue, there came a stage when I was faced with innumerable occasions to hone and master the art and indeed science of archery. There were few young rabbits safe from my eager eye and keen appetite when striding out amongst the bluebells and bracken with my taught bow I can tell you!

Having watched many TV adverts for Strongbow Cider where various archers fire their arrows at a selection of bars, tables and other furniture types associated with places of cider appreciation I am convinced I could do a far better job. Not only could I be of use in drawing attention to the pint of Strongbow Cider itself in the tradition of your well-established adverts but also my presence as the 'Mad, Bald Archer of Storthes Hall Woods' might convince certain publicans to stock more of your product and less of that belonging to the competition. This would doubtless be a novel marketing strategy!

In terms of salary I am reasonably flexible provided I am paid enough to purchase a new tarpaulin for the roof of my woodland shelter and a ball of good quality string. Perhaps we could come to an agreement in terms of a reasonable allocation of cider samples on a weekly or monthly basis also?

I trust that my credentials have persuaded you to consider taking my job application to the next stage and I look forward to hearing from you in the very near future.

Sincerely

Michael A. Lee

HP Bulmer Limited
The Cider Mills, Plough Lane,
Hereford HR4 0LE, England

Telephone +44 (0)1432 352000
Facsimile +44 (0)1432 352084
Web Site www.bulmers.com

Bulmers

Mr M A Lee
Somewhere in West Yorkshire

NEC/YJ   21 September 2001

Dear Mr Lee

Thank you for your entertaining letter applying for the roles of "Archer" with this
Company.

We have, at present, a full complement of skilled Bowmen across the Company but are
always interested in hearing from those who possess this increasingly rare talent. I have
passed your letter to our Marketing Manager in charge of the Strongbow brand and I am
sure that she will be in contact if any suitable opportunities arise.

In the meantime may I urge you to continue to explore the refreshing taste of Strongbow
cider but ask that you refrain from practising your archery after enjoying a pint of two of
the above.

Yours sincerely

Neil Chambers
UK HR Director

TBWA\LONDON

Mr. Michael Lee
Somewhere in
West Yorkshire

November 1st 2001

Dear Mr. Lee,

Many thanks for your interest in Strongbow and your application for the position of 'Archer'.

Unfortunately, we commission a special effects company who use an automated rig for the firing of the Strongbow arrows. This ensures we comply with health and safety regulations, and insurance requirements, on our film shoots. Hence, the position of archer is not currently available.

I do hope you find an alternative opportunity for your archery skills.

Kind regards,

Rebecca Tickle,
Account Director.

cc. Annie Neil
Neil Chambers

TBWA\LONDON LTD
76-80 Whitfield Street
London W1T 4EZ

+44 (0)20 7573 6666 t
+44 (0)20 7573 6667 f
www.tbwa-london.com

**The Managing Director
Sentinel Lightning Protection
        & Earthing Ltd
Unit C
Thornfield Industrial Estate
Hooton Street, off Carlton Road
Nottingham NG3 2NJ**

Dear Sir

I am writing to you a most unusual letter, namely to apply for a job with your company as a 'Lightning Conductor'.

Aged 41, I am at that interesting time of life where half a career in sales has led to my looking at alternative challenges that might better suit my character and abilities whilst offering direction of a rather different nature to the one in which I am presently involved.
In short I am looking for a job with an added degree of excitement and one which would be 'charged' with possibilities.

On Wednesday 15 February 1995 I was struck by lightning during an early evening run on the hilly outskirts of Huddersfield during a thunderstorm. I am filled with awe when I think back to the instant when I watched my own hand and foot illuminate with brilliant white light. Fortunately for me, the long-sleeved running vest and long-legged Ronhill Tracksters that I was wearing at the time were as wet as is conceivably possible due the driving rain that accompanied the storm and I presume that the lightning tracked around my wet garments and earthed through my rubber soled training shoes. The subsequent ECG at the local hospital showed no damage to the heart and there were no burns either. I do, however, sometimes wonder whether a small charge of electricity created short circuits in my cerebral cortex but that is hypothesis rather than proven fact!

In this respect I would be most interested to know whether you might have any requirement for a human lightning conductor provided of course you could supply the equipment to safeguard any personal injury whilst the lightning is actually being conducted. I would be most interested once again to observe the electrical surge of a lightning strike pass safely around my protected self but perhaps in a different location to the one previously.
Perhaps there might be some potential for my deployment, not on the summit of a hill, but at the top of a church steeple, mill chimney or strapped to the wing of a light aircraft in thunderous conditions. The subsequent experience would certainly make interesting reading in terms of an article in the newspapers or as a news feature on TV thus creating some free advertising for your, or should I say 'our' business, and would also safeguard the structure to which I was assigned from high voltage damage. In addition I would have the opportunity to add extra dimensions to my CV and to my overall experience in the wilder side of life.

I trust that you will be interested to take this application to the next stage of the interview process and I look forward to hearing from you in the very near future.

Sincerely

Michael A. Lee

PS In terms of luncheon arrangements I am willing to provide my own bread and toasting fork!

SENTINEL

Nationwide service in design and
installation of Lightning Protection systems,
including Earthing and Testing to B.S. 6651: 1999

**Sentinel Lightning Protection
and Earthing Ltd.**

UNIT C
THORNFIELD INDUSTRIAL ESTATE
HOOTON STREET
NOTTINGHAM NG3 2NJ
Telephone 0115 985 9222
Fax 0115 985 9393
Web Site www.sentinel-lightning.co.uk
E-mail enquiries@lightning-conductors.co.uk

Our ref. SJC/LMF

19th September 2001

Michael A Lee
Somewhere in West Yorkshire

Dear Mr Lee

Further to your letter dated 16th September 2001.

We were most intrigued to hear of your encounter with one of natures most spectacular phenomena, namely an electro-magnetic discharge to earth, or in laymans terms, "LIGHTNING".

Such discharges are of course not unusual in themselves, but it has to be said that seldom are such events witnessed at such close quarters and subsequently reported in detail.

Needless to say, upon hearing of your unusual conductive properties, we immediately set about examining our field of operations in search of a possible opening for your talents, but we were unfortunately unable to isolate such an opening within or normal scope.

However, so unusual are your particular dissipative attributes that we considered expanding our normal scope of operations into the following areas, with the specific aim of creating a previously non-existent position.

A) Radcliffe on Soar Power Station lies directly in the final approach path of aircraft landing at the East Midlands airport, and as such it's 600 foot chimney stack is fitted with the mandatory array of aircraft warning lights, which have been on occasion known to fail during electro-magnetic storms.

This prompted us to examine the possibilities of "renting" you out on an hourly basis, your brief being to stand atop the 600 foot stack, waving a red spotlight at the cockpits of approaching aircraft and holding a large illuminated placard clearly emblazoned with the words "*TEMPORARAY TRAFFIC LIGHTS*", with also the slightly less prominent sub-script "*courtesy of Sentinel Ltd*", together with our telephone and fax numbers.

Unfortunately however, we had trouble getting this idea through the Health and Safety executives risk assessment procedure, since it was the general consensus of opinion within the executive that an unacceptable degree of risk was attached to airline pilots in trying to write down our telephone and fax number whilst attempting to land a large passenger jet during such inclement weather conditions.

№ 9902

Registered No. 2627073

Certificate number 2407/00

Continued......

B) We made representation to the National Association of Fish Farmers with a view to reducing their labour costs for the maintenance of stock ponds.

When a stock pond is due for maintenance, it is often necessary to remove the fish to a holding pond using the "electro-netting" procedure. This involves several staff members wading around for several hours using low voltage shock devices until the large number of fish are removed.

Again, we considered renting you out on an hourly basis, to stand barefoot, somewhere close to the centre of the relatively shallow pond, whilst holding on tightly to a length of steel wire armoured 36kV power cable carrying some 36,000 volts of direct current, thus effectively electrifying the entire pond with a single short voltage pulse.

We were however politely informed that whilst the merits of the speedy removal of stock were obvious, it is nevertheless desirable for at least the bulk of the fish to actually survive the removal process and subsequently be returned ALIVE to the stock pond after maintenance.

It is with regret therefore that at this particular time we are unable to find a suitable outlet for your talents within our current scope of operations.

Rest assured however, that we are actively engaged in the consideration of other options, which at a later date may indeed prove to be profitable for both ourselves and yourself alike.

One option, although in the early stages of the development process, is the one man operation *HUMAN UNDERWATER WELDING SYSTEM* (how long can you hold your breath?), which requires no equipment other than the weighted harness which allows you to sink to the desired depth whilst attached to a high voltage welding cable.

Welding operations will be carried out with "fingertip" accuracy since the necessary charge will be delivered to the weld site by simply touching it with your index finer, and subsequently running said finger around the joint.

In the meantime however, as a possible financially lucrative aside, one wonders if the manufacturers of RON HILL TRACKSTERS have ever considered the thermal and electro-magnetic dissipation properties of their sportswear as a possible selling point, and whether or not they may wish to consider entering into a contract with your goodself, featuring a series of time lapse colour photographs, taken at an incredibly high shutter speed, of yourself in a suitably darkened environment, whilst being subjected to an artificially induced electrical discharge of say in the region of 100kA for a duration of 100 micro-seconds, whilst standing in a bucket of water and wearing RON HILL SPORTSWEAR.

As an advertising aid, or indeed as the main thrust of a campaign aimed at perhaps runners who live in an area with a high concentration of high voltage overhead power lines, the above photographs would surely attract a substantial dividend for the subject of the pictures.

It has to be said that the photographic effect is spectacular, although I must admit that I have only ever seen one such sequence of pictures, taken during a recent execution in America.

For now at least, we shall keep your details on file with a view to possible future contact.

Yours sincerely

S J CARGILL
MANAGER

Himself The Pope
The Vatican
Rome
Italy

Dear Sir

I am writing to you a most unusual letter, namely to apply for the position of 'Fisher King', a role for which I believe the previous incumbent had responsibility to guard that most treasured of ancient objects, the Holy Grail. Since the Grail has been an object of great interest and quest by those within the church for many centuries I thought it appropriate to approach your good self as a leader of the worldwide church is my first point of contact.

As an individual who is reasonably fit in body and mind I believe I would be an ideal candidate for the aforementioned position as it is well within my capacity to offer a degree of physical strength combined with an astute attention as far as general security of the Grail is concerned. Like the original Fisher King I am quite willing to relocate to a castle situated in a remote place surrounded by a sufficient amount of wasteland and, as a highly self-motivated individual, would be most content to undertake my duties in such a challenging and unusual environment. As far as the Grail itself is concerned I have it on good authority by a friend of mine that it has been seen on show in the window of an antique shop in the Glastonbury area of England and is available for a modest price. [I am not entirely sure that the proprietor of the shop realises the value of the object in his possession either materially or more importantly as far as church significance is concerned so it will be best for everyone if ownership changes hands.] I understand that my friend will complete a purchase of the Grail very shortly.

You will doubtless be most interested in my timely enquiry around this vital position and I look forward to hearing from you in the very near future.

Once again may I thank you for your time and consideration.

Sincerely

Michael A. Lee

SECRETARIAT OF STATE

FIRST SECTION · GENERAL AFFAIRS

From the Vatican, 2 October 2001

Dear Mr Lee,

I am directed to acknowledge the letter which you sent to His Holiness Pope John Paul II and I would assure you that the contents have been noted.

His Holiness will remember you in his prayers.

With good wishes, I remain

Yours sincerely,

Monsignor Pedro López Quintana
Assessor

Mr Michael A. Lee
Somewhere in West Yorkshire

Stephen Byers
Minister for Transport, Local
      Government & the Regions
The House of Commons
London

Dear Sir

I am writing to you a most unusual letter, namely to apply for the position with the present government of 'King of the Road' and as Minister for Transport I thought you might be the ideal person to approach in this regard.

Like you, I am a keen fell-walker and in so saying I have spent much time on many occasions travelling to various countryside regions around the UK in order to prowl the hills and mountains of our more scenic regions. Indeed the Yorkshire Dales and the Lake District are favourite haunts of mine when time and a demanding family permit and I like nothing better than to indulge myself in hours of solitary hiking for relaxation and enjoyment.

In this regard, I am sure you will appreciate the time spent anticipating the sense of freedom that precedes these therapeutic expeditions into the hills and dales and the fact that it is often necessary to do so whilst travelling by car or train via our busy motorway, road and rail network.

Similarly, I am sure that you will also be familiar with that legend of travelling stalwarts who not only travelled extensively across the USA for many years but also captured the aforementioned freedom and pure enjoyment of such travel in song, the one and only Boxcar Willie. His rendition of that all-time song 'King of the Road' has inspired me on many occasions in the past in a musical sense and has now fuelled my ambitions for a new job at a time of life when I would relish the chance of facing new challenges and job responsibilities.

As the officially appointed 'King of the Road' I could be employed a three-fold capacity. First, I could act in an advisory capacity to provide best route information for those members of parliament who are taking to the roads and rail for either recreational or indeed business reasons.

Second, I could attend the House of Commons Christmas Party and sing my own version of Boxcar Willies' 'King of the Road' to lift the spirits of all the members and prepare everyone for their seasonal break.

… continued

Finally and most importantly, I could have my craggy self dressed in a similar fashion to Boxcar Willie broadcast on TV and in the national papers as the image of the Department of Transport and provide a figure of familiarity and fondness to help forge rapport between the department and the public. Mine could be the facial focus of your bill-board advertising and letterhead imagery.

Doubtless you will want to spend some time considering me for this exciting role and I look forward to hearing from you in the very near future regards details of how we will take my application to the next stage of the employment process.

Sincerely

M. A. Lee

Michael A. Lee

DTLR
TRANSPORT
LOCAL GOVERNMENT
REGIONS

Teresa Stembridge
PS to Michelle Banks
HR - Customer Service

Department for Transport,
Local Government and the Regions
Zone 5/01
Great Minster House
76 Marsham Street
London
SW1P 4DR

Michael A Lee
Somewhere in West Yorkshire

Direct Line: 020 7944 6041
Divisional Enquiries: 020 7944 6041
Fax: 020 7944 2215
GTN No: 3533
teresa.stembridge@dtlr.gsi.gov.uk

Web Site: www.dtlr.gov.uk

29 November 2001

Dear Mr Lee

I am writing in response to your letter of 16 October 2001, addressed to Stephen Byers.

My apologies for the delay in responding to you – your letter does not appear to have reached the Minister's office until 2 November, and was subsequently passed on to us here in the Human Resources Division for response.

Unfortunately we do not have any vacancies within the Department for the position mentioned in your letter. We will, however, keep your details on file and contact you again should any similar positions become available.

Yours sincerely

Teresa Stembridge

Teresa Stembridge

INVESTOR IN PEOPLE

Document2

Somewhere in West Yorkshire
16 October 2001

The Manager/Director
Jodrell Bank Planetarium
Jodrell Bank Science Centre
Macclesfield
Cheshire

Dear Sir/Madam

I am writing to you a most unusual letter, namely to apply for the position at Jodrell Bank Planetarium of 'The Man in the Moon'.

There have doubtless been millions upon millions of children throughout British history who have been taught by their parents and through countless books that there exists a character called 'The Man in the Moon'. Indeed, as a small child in the 1960s I not only believed in this legendary figure myself, but was quite convinced at the time that I could in fact see this person as I looked at a full moon on a rare, clear night. [Even today I am similarly convinced that such is the case after a few glasses of a good red wine!] It was with significant distress, therefore, that I watched the first human beings land on the moon in 1969 – or so it was portrayed by the Americans – as I wondered if they might frighten off the age-old guardian of our bright night light and somehow change the lunar face for good.

As the present generation of children visit your world-famous planetarium in London there must be a huge expectation for many to catch sight not only of the whirling galaxies, solar flares and planetary wonders but also to see, be it even for a few moments, their familiar friend 'The Man in the Moon.' I would imagine that for a not insignificant few an absence of such a sighting might be grossly disappointing and detrimental to the satisfaction of their visit.

Aged 41, I am an individual with a craggy, cratered face that is suitably rounded and I also have a pair of blue, twinkling eyes with a happy sort of smile to boot. In short I would be an ideal candidate for the role of 'The Man in the Moon' should you decide that such a character be employed forthwith. I am a gregarious individual with a certain enthusiastic eloquence and would be only too happy to provide an informative presentation on the origins, geology and exploration of the moon from my seat high up in the roof of the planetarium to the awe and fascination of the audience below.

Doubtless you will want to take this job application to the next stage of your selection process and in this regard I look forward to hearing from you in the very near future.

Many thanks for your time and consideration.

Sincerely

Michael A. Lee

PS As far as meals are concerned I would anticipate bringing my own packed lunch which usually contains a generous helping of green cheese, and so there would be no need on your part to worry about a food allowance of any kind.

Jodrell Bank
Science Centre & Arboretum

Thursday, 18 October 2001

Michael A Lee,
Somewhere in West Yorkshire

Dear Mr. Lee,

Thank you for your 'most unusual' letter which I read with interest. Currently we do not have any vacancies at the Science Centre and our programme of events when external organisations provide activities, drama workshops etc., are fully booked for 2001/02.

Thank you however for writing to tell us of the unique experience that you could provide.

Yours sincerely,

Sylvia Chaplin
General Manager

Macclesfield Cheshire SK11 9DL
Fax: 01477 571695 Tel: 01477 571339

Administered by The University of Manchester
VAT Registration No. 148581834

Head of Corporate Personnel
Chief Executives Department
Greenwich Borough Council
2nd Floor
29–37 Wellington Street
Woolwich
London SE18 6RA

Dear Sir

I am writing to you a most unusual letter, namely to apply for the position with Greenwich Borough Council of 'Old Father Time' should this become available in the near future.

The name of Greenwich is doubtless one of world renown as far as its' connection with Greenwich Mean Time is concerned and its' association with it marking the very meridian where East officially meets West. I am sure that without such a location of time reference the world might be a far more confused place than it is already and there would be countless individuals involved in endless arguments around the subject of past, present and future time and the setting of various timepieces. The working day of the world population would perhaps begin and end in a variety of unacceptable ways according to the whims and fancies of the employees concerned and lunch hours might be extended indefinitely and without timed discipline. Bars might stay open far too long into the night and small children might never reach their respective schools before the cessation of the days' lessons. Society and its' economy would descend miserably into chaos very quickly indeed.

I am sure that the key reason that our society has not sunk in such a fashion to the dark depths of irretrievable disorder is credit to the legendary figure of timekeeping and temporal management himself, 'Old Father Time'. My great concern, of course, is that being 'Old' may well mean the near-future arrival of the present incumbents' demise and the urgent need for a credible and able replacement. I have certainly in all my years never heard of any replacement of the existing holder of this office and presume he must be approaching retirement or, worse still, due to receive a visit from his cousin The Grim Reaper!

As a 41-year-old fell runner and long-standing member of the Fell Runners Association I am officially recognised by the rules of the organisation as a 'veteran'. Indeed, I have to tell you that my creaking knees and back are in collusion with this definition also, although, needless to say, that my mind is keen and alert and my life expectancy over the next forty years or so significantly positive and optimistic. Add to this the fact that I am actually a father of two small children and also have a 1961 Omega Seamaster watch that keeps exact time if wound up every day and you will understand that I would be an ideal candidate for the role of 'Old Father Time' should a candidate be sought. I am a man who balances prospects with maturity.

Many thanks for your time and consideration as far as this job application is concerned and, although you will no doubt receive many letters of a similar ilk to this each month, I do look forward to hearing from you in the very near future and taking this application to the next stage of the employment process.

I feel confident that we could work efficiently together and maintain the worlds' many endeavours in the timed fashion to which it is accustomed.

Sincerely

Michael A. Lee

Reply to Jim Parrott

Telephone 020-8921-5003

Facsimile 020-8921-5718

email jim.parrott@greenwich.gov.uk.

To Mr M A Lee
Somewhere in
West Yorkshire

Corporate Personnel

Chief Executive's Department

2nd Floor
29-37 Wellington Street
Woolwich
London SE18 6RA

Our Ref JP/cc/H09/1

Your Ref

Date 30 October 2001

Dear Mr Lee

Thank you for your recent application for the position of 'Old Father Time'. Whilst Greenwich Council is proud of its position on the meridian the responsibility for time itself lies with the Royal Observatory and you may wish to pursue your enquiries with them.

However, my understanding is that the current incumbent has achieved unusual longevity and that no vacancy is expected imminently. This may be connected with some blurring of the calendar in relation to the meridian although that might be more readily understandable in the other hemisphere where the meridian becomes the international dateline and at least one hostelry, which claims to lie directly upon it, circumvents local licensing laws by operating three bars in different parts of the building known as yesterday, today and tomorrow.

I also fear that it would be impossible to provide fells in this vicinity. However, I can vouch for the local hills providing a more than adequate challenge a decade, or so, on from formal recognition as a 'veteran'.

With best wishes

Yours sincerely

JIM PARROTT
HEAD OF CORPORATE PERSONNEL

Somewhere in West Yorkshire
22 October 2001

The Manager/Director
Maritime & Coastguard Agency
Spring Place
105 Commercial Road
Southampton SO15 1EG

Dear Sir/Madam

I am writing to you a most unusual letter, namely to apply for the position with the Maritime & Coastguard Agency of 'Iceberg Warden' should such be available either presently or in the near future.

Living in West Yorkshire, I am a 41-year-old sales executive looking to pursue an alternative career pathway that would offer a certain degree of new challenge as well as providing the route to focusing my attention on coastal issues, rather than those pertaining to an inland environment as is my present situation.

Living in the heart of the industrial backwoods you will doubtless sympathise with the shock I felt when I read just last week of the sinking of the Titanic. [The postal service is always a little slower here than in most other British towns!] It occurred to me that in order to avoid a similar tragedy happening in British waters it would surely be of the highest priority to appoint someone to monitor the movement of icebergs and perhaps even paint them in a noticeable luminescent colour so that even at night our brave sailors could see them from a distance as they float precariously around our sea and ocean territory. [The icebergs, that is, not the sailors!]

Although I would certainly require some specialist training to satisfactorily fulfil my duties and responsibilities I can assure you that I would be an ideal candidate for the job. As a geographer I spent much of my youth armed with a trusty watch and sturdy pair of training shoes timing the progress of oranges down stretches of various local Yorkshire streams in order to gauge speed of various rivulets and wild waterways, and hence you can rest assured that the movement of natural phenomenon is not a new concept to me. I am also a dab hand at calculating the possible pathways that moving objects might take given a miscellany of variables and the application of my Physics 'A' Level and natural psychic ability.

Finally, I have had an abundance of painting and decorating experience over the years and would find the painting of roving icebergs a bright and noticeable colour a relatively straight-forward task. I am sure that you will process many letters requesting employment with your well-respected organisation but feel confident that my credentials will convince you to take my application to the next stage of consideration.

Many thanks indeed for your time and I look forward to hearing from you in the near future.

Sincerely

Michael A. Lee

PS Should I be successful in my bid for employment would you provide the cold weather overcoat and mittens or would I be expected to purchase them myself?

Maritime and Coastguard Agency

Bay 3/25
Spring Place
105 Commercial Rd
Southampton
SO15 1EG

TEL: 023 8032 9100
DDI: 023 8032 9277
GTN: 1513 277
FAX: 023 8032 9122
richard_wilson@mcga.gov.uk

Michael A Lee Esq
Somewhere in West Yorkshire

Your ref:

Our ref:

24 October 2001

Dear Mr Lee,

Thank you for your interesting letter about the possibility of employment as an Iceberg Warden.

I am pleased to tell you that the United Kingdom is a signatory to the North Atlantic Ice Patrol Service operated by the United States and Canada. The service uses aerial surveillance to spot icebergs and modern communications and navigation equipment at sea ensures that ships are warned of the dangers.

Against the background of that tried and tested arrangement, we will not need to take up your proposal.

Thank you again for your interest in maritime safety.

Yours sincerely,

Richard Wilson
Head of Strategic Planning

INVESTOR IN PEOPLE

An executive agency of the Department for Transport, Local Government and the Regions

The Manager/Director
Tate Modern
Bankside
London SE1 9TG

Dear Sir/Madam

I am writing to you a most unusual letter, namely to explore the possibilities of the Tate Modern purchasing or exhibiting a series of what I am sure are unique pictures created by none other than a house spider that has taken a shine to living in our home here in West Yorkshire and thus become a recognised 'Northern Exhibitionist'.

Doubtless you recall the recent media coverage of 'Thai Elephant Art' discussing the artistic accomplishments of elephants that had been supplied with canvas, paint and brushes. I believe that these works of art have become very popular and indeed rather chic.

In the same way I am convinced that the many 'spider footprint paintings' we have collected on quality cartridge paper through the colourful wanderings of our very own 'Boris' the house spider would be of huge interest to many people through a wonderful combination of novelty and aesthetic appreciation of fine spider artwork.

Much of the work is at present unframed but should you be interested in either purchasing it or perhaps exhibiting it and selling it on my behalf we could always organise the framing also. I have had a rather clever idea to frame the pictures using a cobweb-like frame made of silk or similar!

I thank you for your time and consideration and look forward to hearing from you in the very near future regards the suitability for taking this idea forward.

Sincerely

M. A. Lee

Michael A. Lee

Bankside
London SE1 9TG

call
+44 (0) 20 7887 8000
fax
+44 (0) 20 7401 5052

visit
www.tate.org.uk

MODERN

Michael A Lee
Somewhere in West Yorkshire

23-11-2001

Dear Michael

Thank you for your recent letter regarding an acquisition.
The Tate Gallery is a British national museum. This means that it is a state organisation
and is funded by the government through the Department of National Heritage.
Acquisitions are decided upon ultimately by the Board of Trustees.
In the field of contemporary art, acquisitions reflect those artists who have already
made a significant contribution and have achieved national or international recognition.
Potential acquisitions of contemporary art generally come from artist's dealers, other
commercial galleries or collectors.
I have enclosed a leaflet which may help you find a more suitable gallery to approach.
Thank you for your interest in the Tate Gallery.
I hope this is helpful.

Yours sincerely

Anita Dalchow
Information Assistant

Somewhere in West Yorkshire
22 November 2001

Nigel Peel
North Cotswold Hunt
The Kennels
Broadway
Worcestershire

Dear Sir

I am writing to you a most unusual letter, namely to apply for the position with the North Cotswold Hunt as 'The Rather Nimble Two-Legged Fox' should this vacancy arise in the near future.

There have, of course, over the last months and years been substantial discussions in many circles, including those of government, around the possibility of a ban on fox-hunting. There are understandably many people outraged at this possibility and should this scenario be realised there would doubtless be many packs of foxhounds and huntsmen disappointed and somewhat redundant as far as their sport is concerned.

However, having thought long and hard about this issue, I believe I could offer a positive solution to your own pack which would, in the event of disappearance of the traditional quarry from the equation, continue to offer you a significant degree of fun whilst maintaining a strong element of serious hunting.

Aged 41, I am a reasonably fit individual with a great love of the countryside and for country sports. Although bald as a coot on the top of my head, I am most remarkable in the thickness and extent of ginger-brown body hair elsewhere on my chest, back, arms and shoulders and from a distance, with shirt removed, have a slight resemblance to our furry friend, the red fox. I am rather crafty by nature and just like Old Foxy I love to eat fresh chicken and rabbit when available, although be it said I usually acquire mine from the butchers shop. Most importantly I am a long-standing member of the Fell Runners Association and, not only am I skilled as far as map and compass work is concerned, but also I can run like the wind when being chased.

In short then my proposal is this: provided the foxhounds are trained to stand back once they have caught me – if indeed they are successful enough to do so – and leave me unravaged, I am perfectly happy to play the part of the fox at any of your future hunts.

Dressed either in a lightweight fox outfit or in my own running attire you could provide me with a five- or ten-minute lead time and I would provide chases such as you have never seen before. You would marvel at the ability I have at negotiating high walls and fences, at hopping over streams, wading rivers and vanishing like some mysterious sprite in the heart of a wooded copse. In the space of a minute I would sprint like a cheetah, lay low like a very low thing and canter gracefully like a thoroughbred horse. I would be a challenge for any pack of hounds and huntsmen no matter how experienced or keen their approach. Finally, I would add an interesting touch to the end of the proceedings by joining the hunt concerned for a pie and a pint at the nearest appropriate hostelry and even provide the team with a fox's perspective of the occasion.

The hunts would be saved, the hounds exercised and thrilled, and the huntsmen offered a day of exceptional sport. Moreover, I would have in these uncertain times a secure role as 'The Rather Nimble Two-Legged Fox'.

I trust that this job application is of interest to you and, thanking you for your time and consideration, I look forward to hearing from you in the near future.

Yours sincerely

M. A. Lee

Michael A. Lee

Kineton Hill
Stow-on-the-Wold
Cheltenham
Gloucestershire
GL54 1EZ

M A Lee Esq

Somewhere in West Yorkshire

1 December 2001

Dear Mr Lee

Thank you so much for your most unusual letter. As you can imagine, the hounds and I are rather hoping that we will not need to take up your offer! My wife and I were particularly struck by your willingness to wear a lightweight fox costume. We felt that, although it would add a splendid touch of authenticity, it might well unnerve the large number of sheep that roam the Cotswold hills.

Once again, thank you very much for your letter, which has brightened up a rather dull start to the hunting season.

Yours sincerely

Nigel Peel .
N D B Peel

Somewhere in West Yorkshire
13 November 2001

David Butterfield
Human Resources Services Manager
Kennett District Council
Brawfort
Bath Road
Devizes
Wiltshire SN10 2AT

Dear Sir

I am writing to you a most unusual letter, namely to apply for the job of 'White Horse Jockey' for one of the many famous white horses present within the Wiltshire Downs area that falls under your own geographical jurisdiction.

Over the years I have heard mentioned on several occasions the names of various white horses such as Westbury, Pewsey, Marlborough and Broad Hinton and can imagine no better place in which they could reside than the beautiful chalk downs of Wiltshire. Never, however, have I heard mention made of either rider or jockey for these wonderful animals and I assume that perhaps the absence of such reference suggests a job opportunity.

I am neither the tallest nor the heaviest person to have walked the streets of West Yorkshire but am agile, keen and nimble as of course all jockeys should be. I am as bald as the proverbial coot and consequently can offer a degree of aerodynamic efficiency when sat in riding position. Even when stationary the wind tends to blow over me rather than against me thus preserving my balance and dignity.

I am also smart and well presented and would offer the many tourists who visit the area in a bid to see the famous white horses a certain enjoyment in the appreciation of quality and the art of dapper dressing.

Although doubtless you will receive many letters of a similar kind to this rest assured that you would find me a candidate of superior standing and an ideal man for the job.

Sincerely

M. A. Lee

Michael A. Lee

KENNET
District Council

Chief Executive: M.J. BODEN, T.D., M.B.A., LL.B.(Hons)
CHIEF EXECUTIVE'S GROUP.
Browfort, Bath Road, Devizes, Wilts. SN10 2AT.
Tel: Devizes (01380) 724911 Ext. **627**
Fax (01380) 720835. DX 42909 www.kennet.gov.uk

Mr M A Lee
Somewhere in West Yorkshire

Please ask for	**Anne Ewing**
Your reference	
Our reference	HR/AE/LM
Date	**11 December 2001**

Dear Mr Lee

Thank you for your letter of 13 November 2001 addressed to Mr Butterfield which, has been passed to me for attention. I apologise for the delay in responding to you, but I wished to discuss your proposal with our Tourism Manager.

You are quite right that we have a number of White Horses within our local area. Whilst your agility and nimbleness would be very useful in order to climb the horses, riding them is not a practical proposition as they are two dimensional.

If however, you would wish to pursue a career in tourism within the local area, our Tourism Manager says that she would be happy to consider you if you would care to let us have further details about yourself.

In the meantime I enclose some information on the White Horses within the area which you may find of interest.

Yours sincerely

Anne Ewing
Principal Human Resources Officer

We use recycled paper products

INVESTOR IN PEOPLE

Somewhere in West Yorkshire
19 November 2001

Head of Personnel
Dudley Metropolitan Borough Council
Council House
Dudley DY1 1HF

Dear Sir/Madam

I am writing to you a most unusual letter, namely to apply for the position or nominal title of 'King of the Castle' at Dudley Castle – and since you are the individual at the Head of the Borough Councils' Department of Personnel, I thought you would be an ideal person to write to in the first instance in this regard.

Aged 41 and experiencing something of a male mid-life crisis, I recently wrote to the Garter King of Arms at the College of Arms in London asking whether I might obtain a title and become a member of the peerage. I have always felt I might have missed being born into the aristocracy by a mere cats whisker but I have nevertheless always carried around with me the intrinsic self-belief in my upper-crust potential. Unfortunately, my wish to become a Duke, Earl, Viscount or Baron is dependant on honours emanating from the crown and sadly there is no emanation forthcoming. Similarly, a Knightage which would bring with it the prefix of 'Sir' is presently and similarly elusive and sad to say I am still as always the ever faithful and aspiring but simply named Mr Lee. Much as I would like to be a Lord, I am not.

Having said this I could not help being influenced and impressed by an experience I had on holiday with my family earlier this year on a Brittany beach when, stood at the very top of a monumental sandcastle that my two fine sons and I had built with great pride, I heard myself uttering the words of the immortal chant: 'I'm the King of the Castle'. At that very moment I felt that the occasion was one of prophetic significance and decided in the blink of a French gnat's eye that indeed my destiny would be to apply for and win the coveted title or even role of 'King of the Castle', dependent, of course, on finding an appropriate castle for which I could be king – even if it meant being a king in spirit and absence rather than necessarily one who resides in the castle itself.

As a reasonably ambitious, intelligent and regal individual I therefore believe I would be an ideal candidate for the role of 'King of Dudley Castle' and I would be very grateful indeed for your time and consideration in this regard.

I am quite happy to relinquish any claims to ownership of any brick, mortar or lands associated with the castle and I would not be particularly discouraged should I be granted the title or role without any royal subjects to whom I could wave. In a similar vein, I have no collateral to bring with me either for the finance of banquets or political purposes, and so there would be as little expected of me as I would expect in return.

Perhaps I could appear at certain formal occasions complete with crown and cloak to introduce an event or function and add to the magic and splendour of the occasion as members of the public say such things as, 'Ee, who would have thought that the King himself would be here; wait until we tell Aunty Edith!' Doubtless you will require a little time to consider my application but I do look forward to hearing from you at a convenient time in the very near future.

Sincerely

M . A . Lee

Michael A. Lee

Andrew Sparke, L.L.B., Chief Executive
Council House, Priory Road, Dudley, West Midlands, DY1 1HF
Tel: (01384) 818181 Fax: (01384) 815226 www.dudley.gov.uk
Minicom Number for the Hearing Impaired (01384) 815273

Your ref: Our ref: Please ask for: Direct Line:

Mr Michael A Lee

Somewhere in West Yorkshire

Dear Mr Lee,

Thank you for your recent application to become King of the Castle at Dudley Council. Thank you for also sharing your life experiences with us. It's gratifying that someone with such a strong sense of purpose, self-belief and regal destiny wishes to be so closely associated with Dudley.

Dudley Council undertakes a range of civic duties and mandatory responsibilities. Whilst our brief is wide ranging, sadly it does not extend to creating Kings, either for Dudley Castle or elsewhere. If it did I'm sure that your commitment and ambition would make you an excellent candidate to fulfil the role. As it is, I am sorry that we must disappoint you.

Please don't be downhearted. Someone of your spirit, determination and evident style is sure to realise an appropriate destiny. If you think of yourself as regal, doubtless regal you will become.

In a gesture of goodwill and in an effort to allay your obvious disappointment we would be delighted to welcome you to Dudley at some point in the future. Whilst we would be unable to offer you official duties, we would be happy to show you a vibrant, confident and exciting Borough and introduce you to some wonderful people who like you, we suspect, do not suffer from taking themselves too seriously.

If you would like to accept our invitation of a day out in Dudley, please contact me on 01384 815228 and I would be delighted to make the arrangements.

Yours sincerely

Jayne Surman

Jayne Surman
Head of Marketing and Communications

INVESTOR IN PEOPLE

Somewhere in West Yorkshire
18 March 2002

The Honourable Mr Howard
Castle Howard
York
North Yorkshire

Dear Sir

I am writing to you a most unusual letter, namely to apply for the position of 'Locum Globe Carrier' during holiday periods at Castle Howard.

Let me explain. Yesterday my wife and I and our two angelic children visited Castle Howard for the first time and enjoyed with great admiration the beauty and opulence of your wonderful house as well as the aesthetic pleasures of your expansive grounds and myriad statues, monuments and fountains.

It was also with tremendous admiration and indeed awe that I observed the actor playing the part of Atlas in the midst of the great fountain holding the zodiac encircled globe on his muscular shoulders without even a hint of movement or fatigue. What a professional!

It occurred to me, however, that there must be periods of time when the house and gardens are open to the public but when this gentleman has time away from the job for holidays or perhaps to receive physiotherapy or shoulder massage. Doubtless therefore this will mean you have a requirement for someone to stand in as a locum Globe Carrier. Herein may lay a job opportunity for me and a solution in staff recruitment for you!

Aged 42, I am a reasonably fit, strong individual with an interest in stately homes and houses, an enjoyment of the great outdoors and a desire to be more involved in classical culture. In short, I would be an ideal candidate for the task of holding up the great globe in the midst of the fountain in a committed, be it motionless manner for the pleasure of your visitors and indeed for your family and your good self.

I am also an affable individual and should there be occasions when small children have become bewildered by the activities of the day or disappointed at parental refusal of an ice-cream treat, they could be brought to the fountain and receive a hearty smile from Atlas himself. Mum could say to her precious son or daughter, 'There is no need for you to cry over a busy day is there? That man has the whole world on his shoulders but still finds cause to smile!'

I am sure that you will receive many letters of this kind on a regular basis and so thank you for your time and kind consideration and I look forward to hearing from you in the very near future.

Sincerely

Michael A. Lee

CASTLE HOWARD

Our Ref: SBGH/SLB/Est.HO.
Date: 21 march 2002

Michael Lee Esq
Somewhere in West Yorkshire

Dear Mr Lee

Thank you for your letter dated 18 March applying for the position of 'Locum Globe Carrier' during holiday periods at Castle Howard.

As you can appreciate, this is indeed a testing position and one that requires great strength, patience and resilience to the cold.

I am sure that our visitors would much enjoy meeting Atlas while he takes his well earned rests in the same way that they are now to find Sir John Vanbrugh, the 5th Earl of Carlisle, and other members of my family stalking the corridors of the house itself.

In order to progress your application further we will need your measurements of the following muscles; Latissimus Dorsi, Deltoids, Teres Majors, Trapezius, Gluteaus Maximus, Biceps Femoris, Gastocnemius. Pectoralis Majors, Biceps Brachii, Brachioradialis, and Rectus Femoris. Furthermore, we will of course require 3 references, and would expect Zeus to provide one of these. How are your relations with Poseidon these days? Can he help!

We would assume that you would provide your own outfit, and please let us know the size and make-up of your entourage.

Yours sincerely

The Hon. Simon Howard

Chairman: The Hon Simon Howard. Tel: +44 (0)1653 648444 Fax: +44 (0)1653 648462
E-mail: sbgh@castlehoward.co.uk

IN CONCLUSION . . .

It is with great pleasure that I can tell you of a recent and rather fitting development in my search for the ideal occupation and that is the offer of an extremely unusual job. As I leave you now to ponder the contents of the book you have just read, you will doubtless be fascinated to learn that I am now the 'Officially Recognised Beast of Bodmin Moor' and on the following page you may read, if you so wish, the terms of the contract I have just accepted. Let us all join together and HOWL with laughter for there is indeed no better tonic for the soul. If anything is to be learned from such lunacy, it is simply 'Where there's a will, there's a way'.

The Best of Bodmin Moor

The Best of Bodmin Moor
Mount Pleasant Farm
Mount
Nr. Bodmin
Cornwall
PL30 4EX

Dear Mr. Lee

The committee of The Best of Bodmin Moor would like to offer you the position of The Beast of Bodmin Moor. It appears that the previous holder of the position has taken an unauthorised sabbatical or has been poached, (we hope the same fate does not befall you).

There are of course a few conditions of employment, which must be met. You must promise not to steal milk from other cat's saucers, leave deposits in people's gardens or 'presents' by their back doors. You may not eat such things as fresh lamb or beef that has not been sourced through the appropriate channels, though as we are currently inundated with rabbits (they cleared out all my carrots and lettuces again!) I'm sure the odd one would not go amiss. You must have up to date vaccination certificates for feline flu and be wormed regularly, only bonafide sickness as diagnosed by our vet would qualify for sick pay, a 'gippy' tummy after a night out on the tiles or fur balls would not suffice.

We reserve the right to terminate your employment forthwith should you make a nuisance of yourself of frighten anyone, severe misconduct will result in incarceration in Newquay zoo for an indeterminate period. Holiday pay would not be appropriate, as this is such a lovely place to live, you could not possibly want one.

Finally the perks of the job include the aforementioned rabbits, as many mice as you can eat, the right to roar wherever and whenever you see fit and a warm welcome in front of the fire at Jamaica Inn.

I hope you feel up to the task and will enjoy becoming the official Beast of Bodmin Moor.

Yours sincerely,

Chairman Best of Bodmin Moor

Promoting the Hidden Heart of Cornwall
www.bodminmoor.co.uk

'The Beast of Bodmin Moor'

THE AUTHOR

MICHAEL A. LEE was born in the celebrated town of Huddersfield shortly before lunch in the December of 1959. At the time his father commented that he looked like a little, wrinkled purple monkey, and this probably had a major influence on the author becoming as far as is known the only human being officially recognised as 'The Beast of Bodmin Moor'.

Graduating in 1981 as one of life's many geographers, Michael (known to his friends as Tony) embarked upon a journey through life as someone not entirely sure what he wanted to do for a living, nor where, nor why, but certain that he preferred his middle name to his first. Having dabbled in the worlds of youth-hostel wardening, house-building, forestry and rolling cloth in a Yorkshire woollen mill, almost twenty years ago our 21st-century Don Quixote settled for a sales career as a temporary measure while an appropriate job presented itself.

Recent years saw the appearance of latent writing skills bubbling to the surface of a rather quirky and esoteric mind when Michael began to apply for a selection of unusual and often non-existent roles for which he is neither qualified nor even vaguely suitable. In this his first book he fails magnificently in his attempts to become the mascot for the Parachute Regiment, Stable Boy for the Four Horses of the Apocalypse and even Jack the Giant Killer [the Second] to name but a few, before he was finally recognised as the animal he is happy to be. Despite everything, he has an understanding wife and two small sons whose patience in tolerating his time spent writing, fell running and waxing lyrical should be recognised at the highest level and presented with medals.

Michael A. Lee is almost 43 years of age and rather bald. He is also a highly acclaimed after dinner and motivational speaker.

ACKNOWLEDGEMENTS

The success of bringing this book to the stage of publishing has been one involving a large slice of creative madness laid out on a sizeable plate of word-processing and served with the cool ice-cream necessity of plentiful organisation. The recipe underlying this sweet dessert, however, has relied far more on two of the most endearing of human qualities: support and encouragement from other people.

The motivation I have had from others is certainly far more important than my own convoluted thinking as I have searched for that unusual job or holiday and on this basis, I would like to recognise a few praiseworthy individuals. First and foremost, a big thank you goes out to my long-suffering wife, who has spent many evenings sitting on her own in the lounge downstairs as I have tapped my Qwerty computer keyboard late into the night upstairs. Thanks, too, to my two fine sons, Tom and George, of whom I am immensely proud and who may have heard a few more stories from the *Thomas the Tank Engine* anthology, had I not disappeared into my office for an hour or two at weekends. Your patience should be recorded in holy books and spoken of at state functions!

Thanks too to all those great friends, who have cried with laughter at both the nonsensical ideas I have asked them about as well as the better ones. I am eternally grateful for my parents' insistence that to speak and write the English language properly in the great land of England has certain cultural and educational advantages. Thanks, Mum; thanks, Dad.

I also raise my glass in gratitude to Melanie Letts, Andy Hodgson, John Wigfield, Mike Fleming, Chris Jowett, Richard and Sarah Lee, Graham Kilner and Josie Brown, Rob and Annika Graham, Robin Sharman, Pete Faulkner, Gerry Williams, Mike Adam, Paul and Ailsa Care, Jim Sedgley, Eamon and Fran McGoldrick, Steve Hemingway, Graham and Suzanne Almack, Sarah Price, John Hawcroft, Steve Arbuthnot, Alison Davies at Mayday Management Limited and my charismatic uncles, Tony and Peter Lee, to name but a few, for substantial encouragement along the way. I would also like to thank Michael Palin for his provision of such a superb foreword and his excellent support of my unusual venture. Even when I thought I had crossed the boundary of sanity you all suggested I continue with my efforts and make it work.

Many thanks to all those individuals who responded to my letters in the spirit in which they were written, for the fun you have provided and for which permission to publish has been granted. Thanks, too, to those who replied without even reading the letters, or who responded in a delightfully mundane and formal fashion. There will indeed be many people cheered and heartened by the humour you have expressed and the words you have written.

Michael A. Lee